The Savvy CFO

Myra Good

Copyright © 2017 Myra Good. All rights reserved. No part of this book can be reproduced in any form without the written permission of the author and its publisher.

Table of Contents

Dedication:..8

Chapter 1: My Story 10
    The Truth Behind Entrepreneurs
    and Money................................13
    Personal Funding............................14
    Family & Friends............................16

Chapter 2: Crowdfunding............................18
    What exactly is Crowdfunding?.20
    Types of Crowdfunding 20
        1.Rewards-Based
    Crowdfunding.................................20
        2.Equity Crowdfunding. 22
        3.Debt-Based
    Crowdfunding 22
        4.Donation Based
    Crowdfunding.................................23

Chapter 3: What Happens When the Bank says No.................................... 29

Chapter 4: Types of Alternative Financing Available..........................44
    Unsecured Business Financing...44

Business Revenue Lending..........49
Merchant Advances........................54
Accounts-Receivable Financing...59
Purchase Order Financing............63
Inventory Financing......................66
401(k) Plan Financing.....................70
Securities Credit Lines...................73
SBA Loans..76
Low-Interest and Long-term
      Business Financing............78
Equipment Financing.....................78
Commercial Real Estate.................81
Private Equity Financing...............83
Book-of-Business Financing.........86

Chapter 5: The Starting Point....................90

Chapter 6: Workpreneur..............................97
Hone Your Craft..............................97
Maximize Your Time......................99
Observe..101
Network...101
Replacing Your Full-Time Income
Before You Leave................................103
The Don'ts..104

Chapter 7: Business Coaches and Advisors..............................108

Chapter 8: Penny Pinching; Tips and Tricks on How to Save Money Running Your Business......................................**121**

    Purchase Used or Gently Worn Items 122
    Be the Jack of All Trades..............122
    Clean Sh!t Yourself........................123
    Collaborate, Don't Compete.......123
    Barter 124
    Get Clear on Your "Needs" vs. "Wants"..127
    Don't Stick to the Sticker Price..127
    Create Systems...............................128
    Separate Your Marketing Dollars......................................128
    Bootstrapping Tips for Entrepreneurs 128

Chapter 9: Door # 3 – Creativity.............**136**

Chapter 10: Let's Win Together...............**151**

Small Business Finance Glassory........**153**

DEDICATION

This book is dedicated to every entrepreneur who's been hit, chin checked and had the wind knocked out of them in this crazy thing we call entrepreneurship. The good thing is, if you can look up and if you can get up, you can move forward to try again.
I'm rooting for you.

I am a small business champion.

I am here to help you bring your dreams out of your head and into the world.
Myra Good

Chapter 1
MY STORY

I love being a small business champion. I also love working with people who are in big corporations and have all the things they need in place. But, it's the person who gets up at six o'clock on a Saturday morning to load up his food truck and sell tacos downtown or the person whose friends are going to Costco to buy a cake even though he runs a cake business that I want to teach how to succeed.

I'm so delighted to be in this place where I am today, but it hasn't always been this way. I used to be in the same place that you may be right now. I started an e-commerce store selling handbags. I had done the research and I knew what I wanted in life was my own handbag line. Not just clutch bags or coin purses, but a whole line of every different type of handbag you can get. Beyond that, I had even bigger dreams. I had a dream to do scarves, gloves and other accessories. I knew that this company was going to be awesome. I even took the names of both my mother and grandmother, Jamison Parker, and made that the name of the company. In this way, there could be a legacy for me and my family from this business. I wanted so badly for it not just to succeed, but to create a legacy that would outlive me. I'm sure many of you can relate to that.

Wholesale boutique stores were at the core of my business. I did pretty well for the first product line. The problem is that product based companies have high upfront costs. There came a time when I got into a place where the money that I had borrowed to fund the company ended up being out of my own personal finances. Rather than being something that was just company based, the money ended up coming out of my own personal credit. So, I ran out of money and even owed money to the finance company.

Because of that, I wasn't able to fund the second ordering round for my business. I also had to sell the entire remaining inventory that I had at a discount to come up with the cash to pay my vendors. All those things took me back to zero just so I could pay off the debts. I never thought I would fail. I always assumed I would succeed. I never thought I would be the person whose business didn't make it. How could this be? I had not only lost all my money, but I had lost my dream. I was lost, and I wasn't sure what was next.

That was the moment I began to look at why these things happened to me. I began to learn and look into personal finance, so I could discover how money actually works for small business people, not for large corporations. As I was learning personal finance and working in that industry, I found out that all my clients were actually small business people who were smart and hardworking. They were out there grinding and hustling, using their own money and fighting for success every day. In that struggle, I understood that failure is actually a part of success. No one comes out of their business unscathed. There are times when the wind is going to get knocked out of you and this is what determines whether you're a hunter or prey. Can you take a leap and keep going?

The Truth Behind Entrepreneurs and Money

Everyone has a different why - the why they talk about. What moves you? Why you do what you do? What brings you to tears? For most of us, it is family. That's what drives us. That's what makes us push when there's no more gas in the engine. That's the one thing that no one talks about - the lonely nights, the self-doubt and the tiredness that you feel all the time that seems never-ending.

So, let's get to the nuts and bolts of it. The real business of entrepreneurship and money is the risk. How much risk are you willing to take? Are you willing to risk it all? I like to believe entrepreneurs all have a crazy side that makes us feel like we're in the clouds. We're the ones who think outside the box. And, one thing we all have in common is that we're going to take risks. It's go big or go home.

I want us to redefine what success looks like. Redefine what you think you want and how to actually get there. Read this book and then always move forward in life with an open mind of what your version of success looks like. This is the truth of entrepreneurs and money.

Personal Funding

First, let's talk about personal funding. I think every entrepreneur has gotten down to their last dollars and used their personal funds to start up their business, form their dream and go after what they think their calling in life is. While there are also some different ways, for now I'll tell you a quick way that you can get some things that you indirectly need.

There are a couple of ways that you can get the things that you indirectly need using personal funds. I think we've all owed someone money and gotten down to our last dollar. We've all felt the strains from debt. No one ever talks about the debt that most entrepreneurs incur, especially in the first year. Don't be fooled by the "I made six figures in six months," or "I made six figures in six days," or "I made a million dollars in 30 days." It's not because those stories are not true, but because those stories are not common.

A lot of times, those people really are making six figures, but not necessarily because of their new business. Keep in mind that sometimes debt may be a part of your journey and that's okay. If you start at the bottom, there's always room for improvement. Never think that you are consumed by your debt or that your debt defines you. Never believe it can't change. It can change. It's just a matter of willing to stay the course.

Family & Friends

This isn't your family's business and they may or may not be your customers, so don't get disappointed if they will not buy from you. Honestly, your family will be the last people to support you. They will also be the first people to claim how much they helped you when your business takes off. Oh the irony, but it is true. They may not be the people that are going to give you money even though your purpose and reason for starting this business is usually for them. That type of hurt can run very deep, but always remember your vision only comes from your eyes.

On this journey your circle of friends will be decrease. Many may not understand why you can't hang out like you used to. Shopping, vacations and movie marathons will be after thoughts. However, you will have friends who will be your biggest supporters. Your friends want to see you succeed. Don't be afraid to ask your friends for help. From shipping online orders to being your cameraman when you need to film content.

For your supportive friends and family, you can ask them to help you with getting the things you need for your business. When I first started my business, when birthdays or holidays come around I always ask gifts that would be used for my business. Open your mouth and share with your family and friends what you need. You'll be pleasantly surprised at who is more than willing to help you rise.

Chapter 2
CROWDFUNDING

Crowdfunding is a $34 billion industry. Crowdfunding allows business owners to obtain low-cost working capital. Entrepreneurs around the country are taking their ideas to the public and getting funding directly from consumers. I believe crowdfunding is the definition of community supporting one another in moving forward. The thing that makes crowdfunding unique is the story. The story is what resonates with the donor. People love the underdog. We want to see the story of success unfold, not just the finished product. According to a report by Massolution, global crowdfunding experienced accelerated growth in 2014, expanding by 167 percent to reach $16.2 billion raised, up from $6.1 billion in 2013. In 2015, the industry is set to more than double once again, on its way to raising $34.4 billion.

Supporters of the crowdfunding approach argue that it allows good ideas which do not fit the pattern required by conventional financiers to break through and attract cash through the wisdom of the crowd. If it does achieve traction in this way, not only can the enterprise secure seed funding to begin its project, but it may also secure evidence of backing from potential customers and benefit from word of mouth promotion in order to reach the fundraising goal. Another potential positive effect is the propensity of groups to "produce an accurate aggregate prediction" about market outcomes as identified by author James Surowiecki in his book The Wisdom of Crowds, thereby placing financial backing behind ventures likely to succeed.

What Exactly is Crowdfunding?

Crowdfunding is the red-headed stepchild of business funding. It goes against all the traditional ways for entrepreneurs to raise capital for their business or to launch a product.

Types of Crowdfunding

1. Rewards-Based Crowdfunding

Give a little something, get something. Rewards-based crowdfunding, also known as non-equity crowdfunding, is when donors are given an item or service for their contributions. Personally, I've seen these types of campaigns work beautifully for product based businesses. If you have an item you are trying to get to market, rewards-based crowdfunding allows you to get the working capital for an initial run, almost like pre-orders. For example, you are a clothing designer and you have run out of personal funds but you want to produce a line for the next season. Let's say you started selling custom pieces on Etsy, and now you would like to open your own e-commerce store with a full line of women's wear. Your need: initial capital to manufacture the product. Customers need: a chance to get to your clothing before others. Exclusivity is what every consumer lives for. We must be the first to have everything. Having an iPhone is okay, being first line to purchase one in your city - SELFIE HALL OF FAME.

Back to the campaign...
The designer would offer a t-shirt for a $50 donation, or a t-shirt and branded poster for a $100 donation. If the funding goals are not met, donors are refunded their money. These types of all-or-nothing campaigns usually gain movement towards the end of the goals when supporters get involved and start to push the campaign for more money. It also allows entrepreneurs to test ideas with the

end consumer and make adjustments before seeking equity partners or investors. In some cases, brands discover they may not want to go the investor route and want to keep 100% ownership of their companies.

2. Equity Crowdfunding

Equity crowdfunding is when donors receive shares of the company. Unlike reward-based crowdfunding, equity crowdfunding occurs during the initial stages of the company. In 2012, the JOBS act was passed which changed a number of laws and regulations, making it easier for startups to go public and to raise capital privately and stay private longer. You must not only produce the product or service for which they are raising capital, but also the equity through the construction of a company.

3. Debt-Based Crowdfunding

Debt-based crowdfunding, also known as Peer-to-Peer or "P2P," started in the UK with Zopa. It came to the US in 2006 with the introduction of Lending Club and Prosper.

Business owners apply online, generally for free, and their application is reviewed and verified by an automated system, which also determines credit risk and interest rate. The reason this is called debt-based is because business owners received a loan against the fund that is made up of securities purchased by investors. The investor makes money from the interest on the unsecured loans.

4. Donation-Based Crowdfunding

Probably the most popular type of crowdfunding is donation based crowdfunding. This is when people come together to raise money for a good cause.

Role of the People

Everyone serves as an agent of the goal, showcasing the project in which they believe in. Sometimes they will become shareholders and add to the growth of the offering. Others will simply play the donor role, geared toward providing help on social projects. When people spread around this information via social media (Facebook, Instagram, LinkedIn, etc.) it creates increased support.

The reason people like to be involved in these types of campaigns is because they feel like they are a part of or responsible for the success of another persons' initiatives. Some people are motivated to participate in crowdfunding campaigns because of the desire to be a part of a communal social initiative, or simply put, to be a part of a new initiative that is something good.

Also, people participate in crowdfunding to see new and interesting products before the public. "See it here first" access often allows donors to participate more intimately with the creation of the product. This is attractive to people who are close with the business owner, i.e. friends or family. It also helps to control project expectations, thus managing the financial agreement between owner and donor.

Crowdfunding platforms are motivated to generate income by drawing worthwhile projects and generous participants. These platforms seek widespread media attention for the projects hosted on their platforms.

Why consider crowdfunding?
Crowdfunding campaigns provide lots of businesses with the opportunity to get the money needed for the business.

Profile - A big part of crowdfunding is showcasing who you are and what you will do to build credibility in the marketplace.

Marketing - Even if people do not donate to your cause, you still reached them. They may have even watched your campaign video or visited your website. The point is, your business and your message reached new people.

Community - Small businesses that are successful at crowdfunding always have great engagement with their audiences. People want to feel like they are part of the movement leading up to the end result of the crowdfunding campaign. Interacting with the donors not only creates a sense of community, but also a cult-following.

Feedback - If your crowdfunding campaign gives donors a sample of the product before it is mass produced, you can receive feedback.

Risks to be aware of:

Reputation - What happens if you don't meet your goal? Will lack of interest from people be a sign that your business idea is a failure? If your campaign not only reaches its goal, but exceeds it, is that an indicator that you should seek investor funding?

Copycats - If your company is in the startup phase and your crowdfunding campaign goes to market, there is always the risk of others taking your idea to market before you. Be careful with how much you reveal about the details of your project.

Overkill - Asking the same donors to repeatedly donate to the same cause will annoy them and they will ultimately stop donating to your campaign.

Fear - As the saying goes, there's always one bad apple that ruins it for everyone. There have been a few cases of people creating crowdfunding campaigns and the company never got off the ground. Currently, there is no regulatory framework, so the likelihood of misuse of funds is high.

Other things to consider:

Time - Engaging with donors via social media, managing investors and getting media attention can be very time consuming for an entrepreneur. Not only are you working in your business handling the daily tasks, but you also have a group of people you need to manage, as well. We know that time is money, so this could also impact your finances.

Lone Ranger syndrome - Do you have a team? Crowdfunding takes support from co-founders and friends to be successful. If you need help, let people know. You'd be surprise who steps up to see you succeed.

Share your story - Make sure that when marketing your campaign, you share your story. People want to root for the underdog. Million Dollar Baby was a box office hit because people loved the story of triumph.

Chapter 3
WHAT HAPPENS WHEN THE BANK SAYS NO

Most entrepreneurs think that because they have bad credit or no collateral, there is no chance of them getting a loan. But in reality, there are actually many different financing options that business owners have and qualify for, even with severe credit challenges or no collateral.

As you already know, banks require good credit and collateral to get approved for business financing. But still, most people only go to their bank when they need money, because it's the only place they know to go. But the most common business bank loan, SBA loans, only account for 1.1% of all business loans (Department of Revenue 2013). The reality is that the big banks are not the suppliers of most business loans.

Even though big banks require good credit and collateral to qualify, many sources don't. The big banks are very conservative. Due to this, they commonly won't lend to businesses in which the business owner has challenged credit or the business has no collateral. But businesses can succeed even if the owner doesn't have perfect credit or doesn't have assets that can be pledged as collateral. Many business loans make really good sense and have low risk based on other factors. So, what types of funding can you get with credit issues or if you lack collateral? Before you know where to go to get money if you have credit problems, you first should know where not to go. These sources might be appealing based on their offers and promotions, but they will not typically lend money to you if you have challenged personal credit. SBA loans, conventional bank financing, private investor money and unsecured financing all have stringent credit requirements.

SBA and other conventional loans are tough to qualify for because the lender and SBA will evaluate all aspects of the business and the business owner for approval. To get approved, all aspects of the business and business owner's personal finances must be near perfect. There is no question that SBA loans are tough to qualify for. This is why, according to the Small Business Lending Index, over 89% of business applications are denied by the big banks.

Many people think that when they have bad credit or lack collateral, a private investor is the best answer. But in reality, investors typically want average credit scores of 650 or higher in most cases, and they almost always want you to pledge some type of collateral. They will also want solid financials for at least two years. This means they'll want to see tax returns showing large net profits that are increasing over time. Think of private money as being for SBA and conventional bank loans that just miss the mark.

"Unsecured" means no collateral is required for approval. No collateral greatly increases a lender's risk. No collateral requirements usually mean it's the quality of credit that determines qualification. Any type of financing that has no collateral requirements and no cash flow requirements will require good credit to qualify.

Revenue based financing, asset based financing, equity financing, crowdfunding, business credit, and unsecured financing using a credit partner/personal guarantor, are all great funding options for any entrepreneur with personal credit issues or those who lack collateral. The truth is, there is a lot of capital out there that business owners can obtain. Most of it isn't available through big banks. The great news is that you can qualify for this massive amount of available financing based on your business strengths, as long as your business has even one strength. The big banks require your entire business and you to be near perfect to get money. But as you're about to discover, there are a lot of other sources who will lend you money, even lots of money, based on just one strength. So, as long as you have a strength to offset your weakness of bad credit or lacking collateral, you can be approved. This is often called compensating factors.

Cash-Flow Based Financing

Many businesses already have a proven concept and have consistently increasing sales. Their strength is that they have shown stability and that they can effectively run a growing business. The risk to the lender is less, as they are established businesses that are growing. How are your sales? Sales are the difference between an untested concept or idea and a real operating business. Will your idea be well received? Do how know how to operate a business? Sales answer these questions. If you have consistent sales, the next question is does the business have existing cash flow proven by bank statements? There are lending options available that only require a quick bank statement review for approval. They won't even need to look at your tax returns. Even if your business shows a loss, you'll still be okay. The next question is does the business have over $60,000 annually received in credit card sales? Does the business have over $120,000 annually going through their bank account? If the answer is yes, then revenue financing or merchant advances might be the perfect funding product.

For this type of cash-flow based financing, you must be in business for at least six months. No startup businesses can qualify. You should have at least 10 monthly deposits or more going through your bank account, not just a few larger deposits. Most of the advertising you see for "bad credit business financing" are these products. These are short term advances of 6-18 months. They are mostly short term at first, such as 3-6 month terms. Then when half is paid down, the lender will lend more money at a longer term, such as 12-18 months. Loan amounts typically go up to $500,000. Usually they will lend 8-12% of your annual revenue, based on your verifiable revenue per your bank statements. For example, a company that has $300,000 in sales might get a $30,000 advance initially. With revenue and merchant financing, 500 credit scores are acceptable and common with this type of lending. Bad credit is okay as long as you are not actively in trouble, such as in a bankruptcy, or have serious recent and unresolved tax liens or judgments. For this type of cash flow based financing, rates of 10-45% are common, depending on risk. Risk factors include industry, time in business, and bank statement details such as number of deposits, average daily balance, NSF charges, amount of deposits monthly and credit quality.

Usually, rates are higher on first advance until you prove yourself to the lender. No tax returns are required, no other income documents are required and no collateral is required. However, you will typically be required to supply a personal guarantee, which is required for almost all business financing that is not accompanied by collateral.

Asset-Based Financing
Asset-based financing, also called collateral-based lending, lends money based on the strength of your collateral. Since your collateral offsets the lender's risk, you can be approved with bad credit and still get really good terms. Common business collateral might include account receivables, inventory and equipment.

With account-receivable financing, you can secure up to 80% of receivables within 24 hours of approval. You must be in business for at least one year and receivables must be from another business. Rates are commonly 1.25-5%.

You can also use your inventory as collateral for financing and securing inventory financing. The minimum inventory loan amount is $150,000 and the general loan to value (cost) is 50%; thus, inventory value would have to be $300,000 to qualify. Rates are normally 2% monthly on the outstanding loan balance. An example is a factory or retail store.

With equipment financing, lenders will undervalue equipment by up to 50% and work with major equipment only. The lender won't combine a bunch of small equipment and first and last month's payments are required to close. Loan amounts are typically available up to $2 million dollars.

Common personal collateral that can qualify for collateral based lending might include a 401(k) and stocks. A 401(k) or IRA can be used to obtain up to 100% financing and rates are usually less than 3%. A retirement plan is created allowing for investment into the corporation. Funds are rolled over into the new plan. The new plan purchases stock in corporation and holds it. The corporation is debt free and cash rich. With securities based lines of credit, you can obtain an advance for up to 70-90% of the value of your stocks and bonds. These work much the same as 401(k) financing with similar terms and qualifications.

Equity Financing and Crowdfunding

With equity financing, you exchange a percentage of ownership in your business or financing, much like on the TV show Shark Tank. Personal credit is not an issue, nor will you need to provide collateral, but equity investors are looking for a tested and proven concept and sales really help approval. You might find some investors to invest in a concept only or an invention. But most will want to see that you have an operating business that's earning money and making profits.

Expect that they're going to want a large piece of the equity. For it to be worth their time to invest, they might want 10-60% ownership of your business. That means they'll be taking a large part of your future earnings, something you'd want to consider before recruiting an investor.

There are lots of websites in which you can obtain crowdfunding for your business. This type of funding gathers money from many people instead of one big investor. If the crowd likes your idea, they may donate money to your project. Much of crowdfunding doesn't need to be paid back and many investors are people you know. If you really look into crowdfunding, you'll find there are all types available.

Some types of crowdfunding sources do want a certain percentage of return; some want a percentage of equity ownership. There are different sources and platforms for different needs, and even unique niches or industries. So, make sure you find the right crowdfunding platform for you before you post a project.

Business Credit and Unsecured Credit

Business credit is a great way to get money, as approvals are not based on personal credit and no collateral is required for approval. Business credit reports usually get started with a few vendor accounts who will initially offer credit. Initial accounts create trade lines and a credit profile and score are established. The company's new profile and score are used to get credit. Newly obtained credit is based on the company's credit per the EIN, not the owner's credit based on the SSN. Personal credit does not matter, as the credit linked to the EIN is used for approval. When you use vendors to build your initial credit, you can then leave your SSN off of the application and can apply for business credit based solely on your EIN at most retail stores. Plus, you can get cash credit also, like high-limit cards with MasterCard and Visa. But building business credit all starts with vendor accounts. Without them, you won't be able to start your credit profile, and that profile being established is the key to getting cash and store credit cards for your business.

Once you find the vendors you want to apply for, apply and use your credit. It takes about 1-3 months for those accounts to report to the business bureaus. Once those accounts are reported, a business credit profile and score are established and that can be used for you to get store credit cards next. Once you have about 10 payment experiences reporting, you can start to get cash credit like Visa and MasterCard accounts. A payment experience is the reporting of an account to one business bureau. So, if an account reports to two bureaus, it would actually count as two payment experiences.

You can get approved for vendor accounts right away that offer credit on Net 30 terms. Once you use those accounts, they are reported, which takes about 30-90 days. At that point, in only 90 days or less, you can use your newly established credit to start to get high-limit store credit cards. Then in about 30-90 days longer, you can be approved for $5,000-10,000 limit cash credit cards that you can use almost anywhere. Due to fast building and approval time, business credit makes a lot of sense for credit challenged entrepreneurs.

Unsecured credit requires no collateral, but it does require good credit. However, even if you have credit issues you can still get approved if you have a good credit partner, or someone who will sign as a guarantor. This person has to have good credit. The guarantor is then liable for the business debt in case that account defaults. Approval amounts range from $10,000 to $150,000. Card limits are equal to what the signer has on their credit now. These accounts do report to the business bureaus in most cases, so they also help build your business credit and they are not reported on the guarantor's personal credit report. Your guarantor will need excellent personal credit to qualify.

Chapter 4

TYPES OF ALTERNATIVE FINANCING AVAILABLE

Unsecured Business Financing

Unsecured Business Financing is perfect for entrepreneurs who are just starting their business, as well as those who are already well established. You can be approved for hundreds-of-thousands of dollars in unsecured financing with no collateral or cash flow requirements.

Unsecured Business Financing is designed to help entrepreneurs get funding based strictly on personal or business credit quality. Lenders will not ask for financials, bank statements, business plans, resumes or any of the other burdensome document requests that most conventional lenders demand.

This type of financing is as close to a no-document program as you can get with business funding. The best part is that you can even be approved with introductory rates as low as 0%, giving this program the best terms in the country.

Easy Qualification Process

Our Unsecured Business Financing program is extremely popular due in part to how easy it is to get approved. To qualify, lenders will look solely at you or your credit partner's personal credit quality. They are looking for very good personal or business credit with little to no derogatory items reporting.

Our lenders will review the credit report to ensure there are no derogatory items on the report. To be approved, you should not have any open collections, late payments, tax liens, judgments or other types of derogatory items reported.

You should also have less than two inquiries on your credit report within the last six months to qualify. You should have established credit, including open revolving accounts now reported on your credit report with balances below 30% of your limits. Lenders typically want to see personal credit scores of at least 700, or business scores of 80 or higher.

Do You Have Credit Issues Now?

If you have good credit, there is an exceptional chance you can be approved for our unsecured financing. But even if you have personal credit issues now and no established business credit, we still might be able to help.

You can qualify for unsecured financing with a personal guarantor. If you have someone, such as a business partner who does have good personal credit, they can apply and qualify for unsecured financing for the business.

Collateral-based financing are perfect for consumers with personal credit challenges. You can get approved with great terms and even if there are severe credit issues. You can also qualify for financing with us if you have been open more than a year and have active cash flow for your business now.

Get Approved with Amazing Terms

Most lenders charge very high interest rates on unsecured financing due to the risk of the business owner not pledging collateral for security. But most of our exclusive unsecured financing offers very low initial introductory interest rates, some as low as 0% for the first 6 months. Rates typically range from 3-15% after the introduction period. The actual rate will depend on risk.

Most unsecured lenders also charge high amounts of points ranging from 12-30%, and they also charge application fees for unsecured financing programs. However it is not uncommon for lenders to offer less than 9.2%, and you only pay them any type of fee if you are approved and have secured your funding.

You can get approved for as much as five times your current highest revolving credit card.

Benefits
0% interest is common for 6-18 months
Business credit can also be used to qualify
24-hour pre-approval
Startup businesses can qualify
True no doc financing program
Application to funding in three weeks or less
No application fees
Credit approvals up to $150,000 per individual
Multiple signers can be approved
No collateral requirements

Approval Amount	$25,000 - $150,000
Credit Quality	Good
Collateral	None Required
Financials	None Required

Business Revenue Lending

Business Revenue Financing is perfect for entrepreneurs who are looking for fast, easy money with few headaches. You can easily be approved for financing as much as $500,000 within 72 hours based on a simple review of your business bank statements.

Revenue Financing is designed to help clients get funding based strictly on their cash flow as verifiable per the business bank statements. Our lenders will not ask for financials, business plans, resumes or any of the other burdensome document requests that most conventional lenders demand.

You can be approved even if your credit score is as low as 500.

Easy Qualification Process

Revenue Financing is one of the easiest, hassle free ways you can obtain business financing.

To determine approval, the lender will review 4-6 months of your bank statements. All the lenders are looking for are consistent deposits showing your annual revenue is $150,000 or higher. They will also verify that you have been in business one year or more.

Lenders are also looking to see that you don't have a lot of non-sufficient funds showing on your bank statements and that you have more than 15 deposits in a month going into your bank account. Basically, they are looking to see that you manage your bank account responsibly and have a decent number of consistent deposits.

If you meet these criteria, you can be approved!

Do You Have Credit Issues Now?

Revenue Financing is perfect for business owners who have credit issues. Lenders are not looking for, nor do they require, good credit to qualify. You can even be approved with severely challenged personal credit and low credit scores.

You can be approved with a personal credit score as low as 500, even if you have recent derogatory items and collections on your credit report. This is one of the best and easiest business financing programs in existence, because you can qualify even if you have personal credit problems.

Fast Funding

You can be pre-approved for Revenue Financing within 24 hours. You can receive your formal approval within 72 hours of submitting your application and you can receive your money in your bank account within seven days or less of applying.

I love this program, partially due to how easy it is to apply and be approved and how fast you receive your funds. This is perfect for business who are in a pinch and need money fast.

Get Money Consistently
Over 85% of our clients come back for even more financing after their initial approvals. Typically, within 3-6 months of approval you will be given an opportunity to get even more money than you obtained before.

All you will need to get approved for the additional funding is a quick review of your last two months of bank statements. Then, you can get your money in your bank account within 72 hours or less.

Revenue Financing helps you rapidly grow and scale your business, as you will have ongoing access to receive more and more funding easily and quickly when you need it!

Benefits

24-hour pre-approval
Loan amounts up to $500,000
Application to funding in seven days or less
Get approved for additional future funding
Easy bank statement review for approval
No application fees
Get approved with bad credit
No collateral requirements
3-18 month financing terms
Get approved for up to 12% of annual revenue

Approval Amount	$5,000 - $50,000
Credit Quality	Bad Credit Accepted
Collateral	None Required
Financials	None Required

Merchant Advances

Merchant Financing is perfect for business owners who accept credit cards and are looking for fast and easy business financing. You can be approved for as much as $500,000 in financing with no collateral and bad credit.

This program is designed to help you get funding based strictly on your cash flow, as verifiable per your business banks statements. Our lenders will not ask for financials, business plans, resumes or any of the other burdensome document requests that most conventional lenders demand.

You can be approved even if your credit scores are as low as 500.

Easy Qualification Process
Merchant Financing is one of the easiest, hassle frees ways you can obtain business financing.

To determine approval, the lender will review 4-6 months of your bank and merchant account statements. All the lenders are looking for is consistent deposits showing your revenue is $50,000 or higher annually. They will also verify that you have been in business six months or more.

Lenders are also looking to see that you do not have many non-sufficient funds showing on your bank statements or low chargebacks on your merchant statements and that you have more than 15 deposits a month going into your bank account.

Basically, all they are looking for is that you manage your bank and merchant accounts responsibly and have a decent number of consistent credit card transaction deposits each month.

Do You Have Credit Issues Now?
Merchant Financing is perfect for business owners who have credit issues. Lenders are not looking for,

nor do they require, good credit to qualify. You can even be approved with severely challenged personal credit and low credit scores.

You can be approved with a personal credit score as low as 500, even if you have recent derogatory items and collections on your credit report. This is one of the best and easiest business financing programs in existence that you can qualify for even if you have personal credit problems.

Fast Funding
You can be pre-approved for Merchant Financing within 24 hours. You can receive your formal approval within 72 hours of submitting your application and you can receive your money in your bank account within seven days or less of applying.

I love this program, partially due to how easy it is to apply and get approved, and how fast you receive your funds!

Get Money Consistently

Over 85% of our clients come back for even more financing after their initial approvals with our Revenue and Merchant Financing programs. Typically, within 3-6 months of approval you will be given an opportunity to get even more money than you obtained before.

All you will need to get approved for the additional funding is a quick review of your last 2 months of bank statements. You can get your money in your bank account within 72 hours or less! We also provide you access to merchant credit lines where you can have consistent access to cash.

Merchant Financing helps you rapidly grow and scale your business, as you will have ongoing access to receive more and more funding easily and quickly when you need it!

Benefits
24-hour pre-approval
Loan amounts up to $500,000

Application to funding in seven days or less

Get approved for additional future funding

Easy merchant statement review for approval

No application fees

Get approved with bad credit

No collateral requirements

Get approved with revenues of $50k or less

Starter programs are also available

3-18 month terms

Get approved for up to one month's revenue

Approval Amount	$5,000 - $250,000
Credit Quality	Bad Credit Accepted
Collateral	None Required
Financials	None Required

Accounts-Receivable Financing

Many businesses wait weeks, even months, to get paid on their outstanding account receivables. This typically creates major cash-flow issues as they provide their goods and services and absorb those costs until they eventually get paid sometimes as many as 90 days later.

With our accounts-receivable financing, you can regularly secure money against receivables in as little as 24 hours. Also, you can get rates less than 2% and financing as high as $20,000,000, even with severely challenged personal credit.

Easy Qualification Process
Accounts-receivable financing is very easy to qualify for, as you won't need financials or good credit to get approved.

To qualify for AR Financing, your business must be open for at least 12 months. The lender will review your existing receivables or purchase orders and will look into the companies that hold your receivables.

If the companies who owe you money have a good history of paying their debts, you can easily be approved, regardless of your personal credit quality.

Do You Have Credit Issues Now?

Accounts Receivable financing is perfect for business owners who have credit issues. Lenders are not looking for, nor do they require, good credit to qualify. You can be approved and advanced 80% of your receivables, even with severely challenged personal credit and low credit scores.

You can be approved with a personal credit score lower than 500, even if you have recent derogatory items and major collections on your credit report. Lenders truly don't care about your personal credit. They care more about the credit of the company who you have the receivables with.

This is one of the best and easiest business financing programs that you can qualify for and get really good terms, even if you have severe personal credit problems.

Fast Funding

After the lenders review your account receivables, you can receive your initial approval and funding in three weeks or less. After you are initially approved, you will be able to get paid on future receivables within 24 hours.

Really Low Rates Regardless of Credit

With AR financing, you can get approved with really low rates, even if you have severe credit challenges. In almost all cases, your rate will be 2% or less, even if your personal credit scores are less than 500.

This means you can get paid tomorrow instead of waiting weeks or months to get paid, and you can do this for less than the cost of accepting a credit card payment from your customers.

There are very few other programs in existence that can give you these low rates if you have severe personal credit challenges.

Benefits
24-hour pre-approval
Receive an advance of 80% of your receivables
Rates less than 2%
Receive other 20% less fee after invoice is paid
Easy account receivables review for approval
No application fees
Get approved with very bad credit
Application to funding in three weeks or less
Get approved with no revenue requirements
Get paid on future receivables in 24 hours

Approval Amount	$10,000 - $20 million
Credit Quality	Bad Credit Accepted
Collateral	Accounts Receivables
Financials	None Required

Purchase Order Financing

Sometimes you might have large orders to fill but don't have or want to use your cash flow to pay for the supplies needed to fulfill those orders. Purchase Order Financing is a short-term financing option that provides capital so you can pay your suppliers upfront and your company doesn't have to deplete cash reserves.

Purchase Order financing allows companies to grow without increased bank debt or selling equity. It also helps you increase market share by ensuring timely deliveries to your customers.

Our areas of expertise include production finance for work in process and Letters of Credit for trade finance. This includes import and export transactions, as well as domestic trade purchases.

Easy Qualification Process
Purchase Order financing is very easy to qualify for, as you will not need financials or good credit to be approved.

In order to approve you, lenders will typically do a quick review of your outstanding purchase orders that need to be filled. If the purchase orders are valid and the suppliers you are dealing with are credible, you can be approved regardless of personal credit history.

Do You Have Credit Issues Now?
Purchase Order financing is perfect for business owners who have credit issues. Lenders are not looking for, nor do they require, good credit to qualify. You can even be approved

with severely challenged personal credit and low credit scores. Financing is very easy to qualify for, as you won't need financials or good credit to get approved.

You can be approved with a personal credit score lower than 500, even if you have recent derogatory items and major collections on your credit report. Lenders truly don't care about your personal credit. They care more about the reputation of your supplier.

This is one of the best and easiest business financing programs in existence that you can qualify for and get really good terms, even if you have severe personal credit problems.

Fast Funding
After the lenders review your purchase orders, you can receive your initial approval and funding in two weeks or less.

Benefits
24-hour pre-approval

Secure funding for as much as 95% of your POs
Easy purchase order review for approval
No application fees
Get approved with very bad credit
Application to funding in two weeks or less
Get approved with no revenue requirements
Rates typically range from 1-4%

Approval Amount	$5,000 - $20,000
Credit Quality	Bad Credit Accepted
Collateral	Purchase Orders
Financials	None Required

Inventory Financing

With inventory financing, you can obtain a low-rate credit line using your current inventory as collateral.

Secure a credit line for 50% of your current inventory value if your inventory is worth $300,000 or more. You can be approved for a line with rates as low as 2-5%, regardless of your personal credit quality.

Easy Qualification Process

Inventory financing is very easy to qualify for, as you won't need financials or good credit to get approved.

To qualify for Inventory Financing, your business must have an existing inventory that is valued over $300,000. The inventory might be of supplies, retail merchandise, materials used to produce your product or other non-obsolescence inventory.

The lender will review your existing inventory and the quality of your inventory management system. If you have inventory that qualifies, you can be approved quickly with just a review of your inventory records.

Do You Have Credit Issues Now?
Inventory Financing is perfect for business owners who have credit issues. Lenders are not looking for, nor do they require, good credit to qualify. You can even be approved for a credit line with rates lower than 5%, even with severely challenged personal credit and low credit scores.

You can be approved with a personal credit score as low as 500, even if you have recent derogatory items and major collections on your credit report.

This is one of the best and easiest business financing programs in existence that you can qualify for and get really good terms, even if you have severe personal credit problems.

Fast Funding
After the lenders review your inventory summaries, you can receive your initial approval and funding in two weeks or less. You will be able to

secure a working-capital credit line to use for whatever purposes you need.

Benefits
24-hour pre-approval
Secure financing of 50% of your inventory value
Easy inventory review for approval
No application fees.
Get approved with very bad credit
Application to funding in two weeks or less
Get approved with no revenue requirements
Rates typically range from 2-5%
Credit-line amounts range from $150,000-500,000

Approval Amount	$150,000 - $10 million
Credit Quality	Bad Credit Accepted
Collateral	Inventory
Financials	None Required

401(k) Plan Financing

401(k) financing offers a powerful and flexible way for new or existing businesses and franchises to leverage assets that are currently in a 401(k) plan or IRA. In as little as two weeks, you can invest a portion of your retirement funds into your business, giving you more control over the performance of your retirement plan assets and the working capital you need for business growth.

Easy Qualification Process

401(k) financing is very easy to qualify for, as you won't need financials or good credit to get approved.

To qualify for 401(k) financing, all the lender will require is a copy of your two most recent 401(k) statements. If your 401(k) has a value over $25,000, you can be approved, even with severely challenged personal credit.

Whatever percent of your 401(k) can be rolled over is the amount of financing you can receive. In many cases, you can secure a low-interest credit line for as much as 50-100% of your current 401(k) value.

Do You Have Credit Issues Now?

401(k) financing is perfect for business owners who have credit issues. Lenders are not looking for, nor do they require, good credit to qualify. You can even be approved for a low-interest credit line with rates lower than 5%, even with severely challenged personal credit and low credit scores.

You can be approved for a credit line with rates as low as 5.25% with a personal credit score as low as 500, even if you have recent derogatory items and major collections on your credit report.

This is one of the best and easiest business financing programs in existence that you can qualify for and get really good terms, even if you have severe personal credit problems.

Fast Funding
After the lenders review your 401(k) statements, you can receive your initial approval and funding in two weeks or less. You will be able to secure a working-capital credit line to use for whatever purposes.

Benefits
24-hour pre-approval
No penalties for roll-over
Easy 401(k) review for approval
No application fees
Get approved with very bad credit
Application to funding in two weeks or less
Get approved with no revenue requirements
Rates of 5.25% are common
Credit-line for 50-100% of 401(k) that can be rolled
Based on proven IRS strategies

Approval Amount	Up to 200%
Credit Quality	Bad Credit Accepted
Collateral	401(k)/IRA
Financials	None Required

Securities Credit Lines

Securities-based financing offers a powerful and flexible way for new or existing businesses and franchises to leverage assets that are currently in stocks or bonds to obtain a low-interest credit line.

In as little as two weeks, you can invest a portion of your stocks or bond into your business, giving you more control over the performance of your retirement plan assets and the working capital you need for business growth.

You can be approved for a low-interest credit line for as much as 70-90% of the value of your securities. Most stocks and bonds are accepted and you keep all of the interest and appreciation from your securities. Plus, there is no pre-payment penalty and your securities remain in your name.

Easy Qualification Process
Securities-based financing is very easy to qualify for, as you won't need financials or good credit to get approved.

To qualify, the lender will require a copy of your two most recent securities statements. If your stocks or bonds have a value over $25,000, you can be approved, even with severely challenged personal credit.

Do You Have Credit Issues Now?
Securities-based financing is perfect for business owners who have credit issues. Lenders are not looking for, nor do they require, good credit to qualify. You can even be approved for a low-interest credit line with, even with severely challenged personal credit and low credit scores.

You can be approved for a credit line with rates as low as 2-5% with a personal credit score as low as 500, even if you have recent derogatory items and major collections on your credit report.
This is one of the best and easiest business financing programs in existence that you can qualify for and get really good terms, even if you have severe personal credit problems.

Fast Funding
After the lenders review your securities statements, you can receive your initial approval and funding in two weeks or less. You will be able to secure a working-capital credit line to use for whatever purposes you need.

Benefits
24-hour pre-approval
No penalties for roll-over
Easy securities review for approval
No application fees
Get approved with very bad credit

Application to funding in two weeks or less
Get approved with no revenue requirements
Rates of 5.25% are common
Credit-line for 70-90% of securities value
Most stocks and bonds accepted
Securities remain in your name
You keep all of the interest from your securities
No pre-payment penalty
You keep 100% of your appreciation

Approval Amount	Up to 90% of Value
Credit Quality	Bad Credit Accepted
Collateral	Stocks, Bonds, Other Securities
Financials	None Required

SBA Loans

Established businesses with tax returns that show good revenues and profitability can get very large sums of funding with Secured Small Business Loans.

If you have positive business tax returns, you should apply for secured government-backed SBA program loans from $250K up to $12,000,000. SBA offers several programs, including 504 and 7a loan programs, which you may qualify for.

SBA programs can be used for many purposes, including purchasing a new business, partner buy-outs, real estate acquisition and working capital.

SBA will require certain documentation to qualify, including business and personal financials, resume and background information, personal and business credit reports, a business plan, bank statements, collateral and other documentation relevant to the transaction.

Approval amounts will vary based on the collateral the business has and the amount of net profit reflected on tax returns. The total time to close these loans is about 2-4 months.

Low-Interest and Long-term Business Financing

SBA loans offer some of the longest payback terms available for business financing. You can secure loans for 10, 15, even 20 years with SBA. Plus, in many cases interest rates are as low as 5-6% on the financing you secure.

Approval Amount	$250,000 - $12 million
Credit Quality	Good Credit Accepted
Collateral	50% of Loan Amount
Financials	Required

Equipment Financing

A recent Gallup survey found that 80% of U.S. businesses lease a portion of their equipment. The list of companies using leasing ranges from the Fortune 500 to the family store.

We offer equipment financing and leasing programs for startup and existing businesses. You can get approved even with challenged credit, you won't need financials to secure equipment financing and approvals take as little as 24 hours.
Easy Qualification Process

You can be approved for equipment financing and leasing with as low as a 640 personal credit score. To approve you, lenders will request details on the equipment you are obtaining or using as collateral to borrow against.

After a quick credit review, you can be approved for as much as $2,000,000 in equipment financing.
Equipment Leasing is Powerful.

With equipment leasing, you receive even more favorable terms than typical business financing programs with even more benefits.

Whether you are a startup business or a well-established business, we have hundreds of equipment lenders who would like to help. You can qualify with only two monthly payments as a down payment.

Rates are affordable and 100% of your interest is tax deductible. Plus, you can get approved for financing ranging from $25,000 to $20,000,000.

Equipment Sale-Leaseback Puts Cash in Your Pocket

Equipment sale-leaseback financing gives you cash using your existing equipment as collateral. If you have valuable pieces of equipment, you can use those as leverage to obtain equipment financing. To qualify, your equipment should be high value, such as $25,000 or more.

If you do have a piece or multiple pieces of valuable equipment, you can then sell those to the lender and they will lease the equipment back to you.

You get cash in your pocket, and you start a lease with the bank with lower payments and interest that is tax deductible.

Benefits
24-hour pre-approval
No application fees
Interest is tax deductible
Application to funding in two weeks or less
Purchase, lease or borrow against existing equipment
Heavy equipment financing available
Loans to $20,000,000
Get approved with average credit

Approval Amount	$150,000 - $10 million
Credit Quality	Bad Credit Accepted
Collateral	Inventory
Financials	None Required

Commercial Real Estate

Commercial Real Estate financing ranges from $75,000 - $20,000,000. This financing can be used for the purchase of property or the refinancing of a property, even if you are doing a cash-out refinance.

Loan-to-values range from 55-65%, depending on the purpose of the loan. Funding programs available include conventional property financing, money for investment properties and hard money loans, bridge loans and loans for the purchase of commercial real estate, plus your clients can also obtain SBA loans.

With commercial real estate financing, you can acquire funding for general or medical/dental offices, industrial facilities, light manufacturing buildings, mixed-use properties, commercial condominiums, auto dealerships, light auto services, daycares, assisted living facilities, entertainment venues, multi-family properties, retail warehouses, self-storage facilities and more.

Private Equity Financing

If you have collateral, average credit and positive tax returns, you can be approved with many private investors at very good loan terms.

With our private money sources, you won't be required to give up any percentage of ownership equity in your business. You retain full control and are still able to obtain private investor funding, even when your bank says no.

Awesome Terms

You can obtain private money financing with much the same terms as conventional bank loans. Rates vary based on risk, typically ranging from 5-18%. You can get approved for long-term loans of 5 years, 10 years, or longer, or you can get your funding through a working capital credit line that you can access and use anytime you need it.

Easy to Get Approved

There are three main elements private investors look for in order to approve you for funding. Firstly, lenders want to see that you have tax returns that reflect a profit. They will also verify that your sales and profits are increasing from year-to-year. Lenders look at these qualities as signs of a healthy company worthy of long-term investment.

Secondly, lenders will verify that you have average credit. You can be approved with credit scores as low as 640, as long as you don't have any severe negative credit items on your report that are recent.

Lastly, to get approved, you should have collateral. Unlike many conventional and SBA loans that require nearly 100% collateral for what you are borrowing, with our private sources you can be approved with collateral equivalent to 20% of what you are borrowing.

Collateral can be liquid cash, stocks, bonds, 401(k), IRAs, commercial real estate or other types of viable business collateral.

Get Approved When Banks Say No

Private money financing is often called SBA fall out, as it typically helps those who cannot get approved for conventional SBA financing. SBA loans have very stringent qualifying requirements - so stringent that nearly 90% of applications are denied.

With private money financing, your business does not need to be perfect, nor do you need to supply the extensive documentation that lenders typically demand. You can get approved with just a quick review of your tax returns, credit and bank statements.

Unlike conventional financing, you don't need good credit; average credit will suffice. You don't need collateral valued at 100% of what you are borrowing like conventional financing; you can get approved with as little as 20%.

You can secure private money financing without most of the headaches and limitations that are common with conventional business financing.

Benefits
Loans from $100,000 to $20,000,000
No application fees
Get approved with average credit
Low collateral requirements
72-hour pre-approval
Rates of 5-18% based on risk
Get approved when banks say no
Credit lines and loans available

Book-of-Business Financing

Insurance agents can obtain low-interest, long-term financing using renewable commissions as collateral. This program is the best program available for insurance agents regarding approval requirements and approval terms.

You can be approved for a 3 to 10 year loan or credit line for your insurance business, even if you have average credit. All you truly need to qualify is a book-of-business of renewable commissions. You can even use the book-of-business for the insurance agency you are buying as collateral to get approved.

Easy to Get Approved

Insurance agents rave about how easy this program is to qualify for. The lenders are mainly looking to ensure you have a viable book of renewable commissions for your insurance agency. If you do, you can be approved, even with a 520 personal credit score.

You can secure as much as 120% of the surrender value of your renewable commissions. Most agencies can qualify, excluding State Farm. All you need for approval is a complete application and breakdown of your renewables.

You can rate as low as 4% over the Prime rate and you can get loan terms as long as 10 years, helping keep your payments low.

Get Approved when Banks Say No
Book-of-business financing is the absolute best long-term solution for insurance agents who can't secure SBA, conventional loan financing.

With book-of-business financing, your business doesn't need to be perfect, nor do you need to supply the extensive documentation that lenders typically demand. You can get approved with just a quick review of your credit and renewable commission breakdown.

Unlike conventional financing, you don't need good credit. You can be approved even with severely challenged personal credit and scores as low as 520. Lenders are actually more interested in you supplying three solid references than they are in you having good credit.

Benefits
Use book-of-business of renewable commissions to qualify
No application fees
Get approved with bad credit
No other collateral requirements
72-hour pre-approval
Rates of 4-9% plus prime based on risk
Get approved when banks say no
Credit lines and loans available
Secure as much as 120% of commission surrender value
Can be used to purchase an agency

Chapter 5

THE STARTING POINT

According to the Census data, more than 40% of all small businesses started up for less than $5,000. 6-4% percent of entrepreneurs in a recent Intuit survey started with less than $10,000.

Do you know how much money you need?

Before seeking any funding or asking your family and friends for money, you need to answer the following questions:

What stage of development are you currently at? Do you need money to start up or grow your business to the next level? Naturally, a lender will be more generous with a business that is 5 years old that is already making revenue (notice I did not say already making profit) versus a startup company.

Is your business seasonal? This is important for lenders to know because seasonal businesses will have shorter payback periods for loans.

How much of your own money are you willing to put up? Be sure to answer this question honestly. If you really don't want to use your own money, fine, but don't mislead others into thinking if they give you $50,000 you will match them. Be honest with yourself and others.

What are your business risks? Every business has risks, however small or large. Identify them and decide how you plan to deal with them.

What is the state of your industry overall? The state of your industry will have an influence on how much lenders are willing to give. Industries that are not affected by recessions always get better lending terms. Some industries include: alcohol, funeral services, asset recovery, junk removal, etc.

What is your urgent need? This is the one thing the money is most needed for. If you need money for multiple things, decide on two things that will result in income generation.

Who's on your team? I know some of you are saying to yourselves, "I'm just getting started. I have not hired anyone." Before you receive any type of funding, know who will execute these tasks. They do not have to be a paid employee, but at least have a list of people or companies that will get the job done.

What is your business plan? Depending on what type of funding you are seeking, a business plan may or may not be necessary. Just in case, I would advise that you have one available if requested.

Take the whole pie. When requesting a small business line of credit, always ask for more than you need. Limit your calories, never your lines of credit.

"Make a budget." This is the dumbest statement for anyone to say. The reality is, when you are starting a business, the budget is simple: This product or service costs X. How do I get the money for it? It's difficult to create a budget for a startup because you really don't know the costs. Yes, you can estimate a few things like office supplies, a web designer and $50 for business cards. But no one can you tell that you'll have to pay the t-shirt printer again because they messed up the first round of t-shirts. No one has a line item in the budget for the Facebook ads, even after you've already spent $1500 on ads that didn't bring any traffic. No one told you that your budget for vendor fairs downtown were useless because your customers are shopping in boutiques and a wholesale business to business model is what works for your business.

The point is that you don't know what you don't know. The only way to find out what works for your business is to get out there and do it. Anyone who tells you they started a business and managed to stay within budget is a liar. Hear their story, activate your side eye and move your feet to walk away.

This is why my chapter on coaches is so important. There are so many business coaches who have never owned any other business other than their current coaching practice that say this bullsh*t every day.

However, let's break down some small business expenses by type. It's important to understand the different types of expenses so you are aware of them.

Expenses: costs involved in preparing to open a business. This includes costs related to market research, trainings (in person and online), consulting services from any professional, accountants, lawyers, etc. (Note, if you decide not to open your business after all the research is done, those expenses are no longer deductible and considered personal costs.)

Capital Expenditures (capital spending): One-time costs to purchase assets such as buildings, equipment and vehicles.

Operation (Non-manufacturing) Expenses: These are expenses incurred during day-to-day operations. This includes things like rent, payroll, office supplies, sales commissions, employees, transportation and travel, etc. If you don't know what your operation expenses are, you can talk to other business owners in your industry to get an estimate. If the costs seem too high, take another look at them and find ways to eliminate or reduce costs. If you need meeting space or space to work from, consider co-working spaces or serviced office space. I cover more of these techniques in Chapter

Chapter 6
WORKPRENEUR

The workpreneur, or parallelpreneur as some may call it, is someone who is working full time while starting a business. You are just starting your business but you need to continue working because your business is not yet profitable or making enough money for you to leave your job. Everyone has their reasons for staying in "cubicle nation," but the reality is that you need a roof over your head, the lights on and food in your belly so that you can start your business.
Below are some ways to make sure you make the best of this time of transition.

Hone your craft
If you want to be an author, write articles, e-books and books. Then,

start writing at work. You can volunteer to write team newsletters or create paper documents if your work is technical in nature. This is a good opportunity for you to hone your writing style and get feedback. If you work for a large company, you can also do this for their employee diversity groups such Women's Council, African-American, or Hispanic groups. The point is to start writing and get feedback on your work.

If your desire is to do speaking/presenting, there are 2 ways I've personally seen this done in a corporate environment that work amazingly well.

The first option is presenting within your team. Managers look good to their directors by showing they are developing their teams. Most managers are too busy to actually take the time to plan and execute this task. Pick a topic, something work related like showing co-workers how to use SharePoint, Microsoft Access or another tool. Other topics could be on team building or how to communicate effectively. Prepare a 20 minute presentation and present this idea to your manager. Show how this presentation aligns with their yearly goals of personal development for their team members. Most managers will not say no to this because this will make them look like superstars amongst their peers who report to the same director.

A second option is to reach out to Human Resources. Find out who the education trainers are in the HR department. Inquire about opportunities on hosting trainings for fellow employees. If you work in a group that services other parts of the company, you can create workshops catering to that audience, as well.

Maximize your time
If you have to work on business after work, make it a goal to never bring work home. During the work day, it can be tempting to stand around chit-

chatting and talking about peas and rice with co-workers. For my readers who are not from the South, talking about "peas and rice" simply means talking about absolutely nothing. It can be tempting to go out to lunch with the sales reps that are treating you to two hour lunches at high-end restaurants. Don't fall for it. During this season of your life, your focus is on building your business. The only way you can do this effectively is if you make the most of your time. Bring your lunch, eat at your desk and focus on getting stuff done.

Now, some people might disagree with me here because they'll say, "you need to socialize with your team" and "be a team player." I say, be committed to your goals and remember your why. Note, I'm not telling you to be anti-social by any means, but watercooler talk is much like watching TV. Neither activity will bring you closer to full-time entrepreneurship.

Observe
Learn from the situations around you. Now that you are an entrepreneur, you should be looking at everything through the eyes of a business owner. How are people hired and fired at your job? Does management take their time hiring the right candidate or do they just put someone in the seat and try to make it work? Will you hire employees or just outsource work to get done on an as-needed basis?

How does this company work internally? What processes will work for your business on a small scale? What makes your employer successful? What is their USP, Unique Selling Proposition? Why do customers keep coming back again and again? Also, consider the lifestyles of upper management. Are they able to delegate tasks so they can work on their business not in their business?

Network
Keep note of the co-worker that's always talking about the latest the tech gadget or the best software. He

might be interested in tweaking your website for a few extra dollars. Get to know the lady in accounting. She may be a QuickBooks pro and willing to teach you how to use it for your business.

Overall, whatever you do while working full time, make sure you set measurable goals and timelines. Treat your business like a project, just like at work. What is the schedule for set up, launch and execution? Do you have a set amount of time of when you'll be ready to leave your full-time job? The best way to create this plan is to consider two things: the amount of money it would take for your business to make for you to be full-time and the amount of time you are willing to continue to work a job. For some, this may be two different time frames. Some of you work in horrible, rude and outright disrespectful environments that have affected not only your physical health, but your emotional health. For you, waiting until your business is profitable will not work. I would suggest that you change to a less toxic work environment with a smaller workload and continue working for the steady income.

Replacing Your Full-Time Income Before You Leave

There is no set formula to this because there are so many contributing factors - married vs. single, parents vs. no kids, self-sufficient parents vs. elderly parents. Also, it depends on the type of business you have. If you have an ecommerce store, you can sell items on your website while sleeping. A business that requires a door-to-door sales model may take more time to reach those financial goals, because you have to work around your work schedule to meet those clients. (Side note: meeting clients outside the normal 8-5 business hours could work in your favor. Who wouldn't want to receive a service without having to take off work? That could be a great selling point to customers.) However, working may be holding you back from reaching those goals. It's a double-edged sword. You can't make more money in business because you are at work. But you can't afford to leave to work because you're not making money in your business. It's a difficult spot to be in and it's completely a personal choice.

The Don'ts

Don't use any company equipment or supplies. This is a sure-fire way to get fired! Even if your work environment is such that they don't mind you using it, do not. Draw a hard line between your job and your business. I wouldn't even check personal email on a company laptop. This includes printing, as well. Printed non-company related emails, documents, etc., could get in the hands of the wrong person.

Don't forget to take time out to recharge. Working full time and starting a business will be draining. That is one thing I can guarantee. Taking time to step away from work and business will allow you to come to your business with a fresh mind and renewed energy.

Motivational Moment
This is probably the only part of this book where I'll give some sort of motivational, inspirational, empowerment advice.

The truth is you hate your job. The truth is also that you need that check. There are days that you sit in the parking lot trying to come up with one reason that you should walk in. You no longer have the desire to work for someone else, and the only reason you keep going back day after day, week after week, is that you have bills. You hate the work. You hate the people. You hate the coffee in the break room, but you drink it because it's free. Take a deep breath and keep pushing. Remember that this is just a means to an end. The purpose of your job is to fund your dream. That's the mantra. That is the goal.
While you are working and building your business at the same time, you

will need to master time management. This is non-negotiable. Your schedule will need to change. This may mean getting up early to go to the gym before work instead of after work, or staying in on Friday and Saturday night instead of going out with family or friends. TV will be a luxury or serve as background noise while you work on things like your marketing strategy, social media or website. Starting out working full time while building your business at night can be a blessing because it forces to you learn discipline. This is why it's so important to focus while you're at work: you need your personal time to build your dream.

"Hustle. Grind. Sleep is for Suckers." This is total crap and completely unnecessary to start a business. Be smart with your time and develop ways to stay focused. Exercise and sleep are essential to being successful in life. I don't know who made it cool to be living off of two hours of sleep and drinking caffeinated drinks to get through the day. Those social media memes may be well-meaning, but by no means should anyone be exhausting themselves to that extent. There is no such thing as overnight success. Proper rest allows you to operate with a clear mind to create fresh ideas and strategies. Eating healthy keeps you alert and your energy levels high. I personally like to set monthly goals and then break them down into weekly goals and daily tasks. Do something every day to move your business forward. Some days, that's just finding time to respond to one email. Do something, no matter how small.

Chapter 7
BUSINESS COACHES AND ADVISORS

Because we are in the age of social media and have greater accessibility to others around the world, coaches are more readily available to small-business owners. Instead of going it alone, business owners are reaching out to business mentors, coaches and advisors for guidance in various areas in their business now more than ever. They can provide help from idea conception to selling or closing a business.

Some of you may think, what's the point of getting a business coach or advisor? Consulting with someone who has already traveled the road you are going down is always wise. However, I use the words coach or advisor because those usually come with a fee.

Let's define business coach vs. business mentor.

Business Coach - someone you pay to consult you about your business with the expectations that, with guidance and execution, your business will improve in an outlined area, i.e. sales will increase, more exposure or re-design of brand or visual appeal.

Business Mentor - someone you admire or want to connect with without having any expectations of them helping you in your business.
Business Mentors can be tricky because there is no guaranteed outcome of what you will get from them. Oftentimes, mentors are asked questions for guidance, but not on a consistent level of availability. Instead they are more like let-me-pick-your-brain types of questions. You may only talk with your mentor once every 6-8 weeks. Or you will communicate on an

as-needed basis. Mentor-mentee relationships can run the gamut, because some mentors can be like a Big Brother/Big Sister type of relationship, and other mentor relationships are strictly business. If you are in business, I do think it's wise to have a mentor and a business coach. As entrepreneurs, we know the most valuable thing we have is time. "Let me pick your brain" is the biggest insult to another entrepreneur. That's why every entrepreneur should have a business coach or advisor. If you do have questions that you would like to ask them, ask for a consultation.

Business Coach - necessary for every small-business owner, regardless of how long you have been in business. The purpose of the business coach is to help guide you away from pitfalls and fast track your path to success. Ultimately, the end result should be an increase in profits or a decrease in expenses or time.

Experience of a Business Coach

Some might not agree with me, but I believe that a business coach should have experience in business other than their current coaching practice. What you need coaching in will determine the type of experience you need to require from your business coach. For example, if your need is marketing, a marketing and branding coach would be fine, regardless of the industry your business is in. However, I would recommend that your coach have experience within your industry. How long have they been in business? How many other businesses have they run before this one? I would also ask for referrals or to speak with one of their current clients.

How Business Coaches and Advisors Help You Make Money

Profit Strategy - Are you struggling financially? Are you using personal funds to pay for business expenses? A business coach should assist with identifying areas of your business that are not profitable. Your business coach should provide a solution about what you need to do to eliminate those roadblocks.

Marketing/Branding - If you don't know who your target customers are and how to appeal to them, that is limiting your business success. Creating a marketing plan and getting clarity on your brand will, ultimately, increase your bottom line.

Business structure and productivity - One of the best things about hiring a business coach is that they can see your business from a different perspective. Coaches will look at how your business is structured and suggest ways to make sure you are able to work on your business as an owner instead of in your business like an employee. Coaches may suggest hiring employees or outsourcing non-income generating tasks so that you can focus on things that result in income.

Mindset - Self-limiting beliefs can have a great effect on your business. Many people start businesses with employee mindsets, thinking that companies can make too much money and that CEOs can make too much money. Sometimes entrepreneurs don't really think about profits at all. They base prices off what they would pay as a consumer, instead of setting prices based on how to sustain a profitable business.

How to Find a Business Coach

Referrals - Ask other people in your industry. Reach out to other entrepreneurs you know. I prefer personal references, rather than just searching Google. If you know the person, most people will be very honest with you. Be sure to ask detailed questions like: How was the program designed? Did you have direct access to the coach? Some coaching programs are fully automated and the clients never have any contact with the coach. Did you do everything the coach prescribed? This is to gauge this person's review of the experience. If they didn't do the work and tell you the program sucked, take their review with a grain of salt, because they didn't truly complete the course. You could also be talking to a course junkie. (Course junkie: someone who loves signing up for programs, but never stays long enough to actually complete them.) You want to ask probing questions, especially if this is your first program. I want you to have a good experience the first time.

Coaching on your level - Take an assessment of your business. If you are a "team of me," a one-man operation, and have been in business just six months, hiring a business coach that services million dollar businesses is not a good idea. You want to take an honest assessment of your business and your skills as an owner to choose a coaching program. There are various types of business coaches that work with businesses of various sizes and stages of maturity. Find a coach that has a stellar track record of consulting businesses at your level. If you are not a good match for the level of coaching you need, an ethical coach will not take you on as a client. But don't fret. They may have some recommendations of other coaches, maybe even someone currently in one of their coaching programs that would be better suited for your needs.

Personality Match - Just like any relationship, you need to make sure you and your coach can work together. Some coaches are easy breezy, laissez faire types that give you advice and do not expect you to execute or don't hold you accountable. Other coaches are result-driven and want to see you taking the steps to grow your business. They pull no punches and they want to see results from their coaching. These types of coaches highly value their talents and will not tolerate any slackers. For some people, this may be too much. If you enjoy just getting guidance and implementing later, these bull dog coaches are not for you. However, some people need a tough coach to motivate them to make drastic changes in their business. If you are at a "whatever it takes" point in your business, you will do well with a bulldog business coach.

The Neither Choice

If you cannot find a mentor and are not interested in one-on-one coaching, group coaching or mastermind coaching is another great option.

Group coaching is when you are consulted by a business coach in a group setting. Mastermind can be the same as group coaching, but at a more in-depth level. Masterminds can be very selective in who they allow in. However, with the selectivity of masterminds, you are almost guaranteed to get exactly what you are looking to gain out of them. Beware, like bulldog coaches, masterminds are not for the weak at heart. Everyone in the group must hold their weight and the other members are looking to uphold a certain expectation of the group. Due to the high level of expectations, the cost of participating in a mastermind can be significantly higher than other business coaching programs.

Three things that masterminds provide:

Support - Entrepreneurs need to know that they are not on this journey alone. Many times, entrepreneurs feel alone because their friends and family are either unsupportive or they just have never owned a business themselves. So, their understanding of your daily struggles as an entrepreneur is limited. Being in a group with individuals who can understand your wins, struggles and failures is essential. Being in a supportive community of likeminded individuals will allow you to bounce ideas around, solve difficult situations and, most importantly, allow you to grow.

Connection - Positioning yourself with a group of entrepreneurs will always be good for your network. Whether the group is formed based on having the same business coach or putting together a mastermind of your own, connecting with other business owners in an intimate setting is a positive thing.

Network - As the saying goes, your net worth is your network. Masterminds prove this saying to be true every time. Even if your mastermind is a group of entrepreneurs from unrelated industries, referrals can come from the most surprising places. When networking, never dismiss or ignore someone because you don't think they can help you. People not only do business with people they like, they refer people they like. Considering yourself "better than" or "above the rest" has never sustained long term business success. Sure, you may get away with it for a little while, but ultimately your revenue will suffer. Remember the story in the Bible about David and Goliath. Don't let the seemingly little guy be the cause of your downfall.

Coaches Do Not Provide Therapy

Coaches, unless licensed, are not for therapy. Yes, some business coaches do focus on breakthroughs for money mindset, emotional setbacks, limiting beliefs about success, etc. However, if you are dealing with greater issues, I encourage you to seek professional help. If you find yourself emotionally venting consistently to your coach about unrelated issues, having extreme reactions to constructive criticism or cannot make any progress and continually seek out the same service, you may not be ready. Before you can receive any type of coaching, please make sure you are mentally and emotionally ready.

A business coach is always an asset to the small-business owner business.

Chapter 8
PENNY PINCHING: TIPS AND TRICKS ON HOW TO SAVE MONEY RUNNING YOUR BUSINESS

In lending, I speak about laying the foundation to qualify for lending and additional business credit. However, we all know that running a business is expensive, especially in the early stages. If you are a small-business owner, there are steps you can take to save money, from bartering with other small-business owners to DIY projects.

Let's discuss some ways to not only save money for business, but avoid unnecessary expenses.

Purchase used or gently worn items.
Equipment costs can seem like an unavoidable expense for a startup, especially if your top priority is to provide the best product and service for your customers. But is the latest model of equipment really needed to achieve the results you desire? Can anyone really tell the difference between the most recent model of equipment versus the current model? Tip: contact the big-name chain stores and inquire about any equipment that is being discounted or models that are being phased out. The discounted rates these stores offer will save you hundreds, sometimes even thousands.

Be the Jack of all trades.
Not only are you bringing your genius to the work, but you also know how to repair equipment. With most equipment, you can (1) find a repair manual or (2) find someone on YouTube who has already made a video on how to solve your problem. If you are in the food service, real estate

or property management industries, you can save lots of money by attempting to cut the middle man and fix things yourself.

Clean sh!t yourself.
Cleanup is an unavoidable part of running a small business. Don't get caught up in the glitz and glamour of running your small business and think you're too good to hire help. Hiring a custodial staff to take care of the day to day operational cleaning is also often an unnecessary expense. Basic custodial duties can be handled as they arise or as part of the shift work of all employees. Train your staff on how to give your shop or your vacant apartment the white glove treatment.

Once everyone knows the protocols, upkeep becomes routine and can be spread across employees so that no one carries too much responsibility for cleaning

Collaborate, don't compete.

One of the biggest advantages that large companies have over small ones is their ability to buy in bulk, and not just bulk like we all get at Costco, but really big orders that are significantly discounted. Unfortunately, small businesses are the ones who tend to have less disposable income and need that discount more, but often they don't qualify. There's an easy solution to this problem.

If your business is struggling to place large enough orders to fully benefit from cost cutting discounts, try collaborating with other companies to place group orders. This is when it really helps to know your competition, because for these purposes, they might not be your competition at all. Rather, companies that are in the same industry are more likely to need the same supplies. Chat up the other local companies and see what other small businesses might make good partners for bulk ordering.

Barter.

Many of us forget that barter is a legitimate form of exchange. We simply don't live in a society that prioritizes the exchange of goods and services for other items of equal value, or really for anything other than money. However, if you're a small business, bartering can be a really valuable cost-cutting tool. Your expenses for a service are less than what you charge customers. Take advantage of this fact and see who might be willing to make a fair exchange.

For example, maybe you really never learned those repair skills because you're a caterer and that just isn't in the cards. Is there a local handyman who might need a party catered that you could work with? Could you exchange landscaping services for some locally made baked goods? With barter, the possibilities are endless. This is creative cost-cutting at its finest.

Sometimes the best way to keep costs down as a small-business owner is to accept certain limitations. You may not be able to get that new espresso machine this quarter because sales aren't high enough. By doing your research, making a budget and sticking to it, you set yourself up for financial success. It's the business equivalent of living within your means. Try practicing these five strategies for saving money, and watch your bottom line grow.

Do you cringe when you hear the words "cut costs?" Do you have more money going out than you have coming into your business? If so, it may be time to consider money-saving measures to rejuvenate your bottom line.

If you're unsure where to start, thirteen entrepreneurs share their recommended cost-cutting tips to help you gain control of your finances and work smarter from the ground up.

Get clear on your "needs" vs. "wants."
By focusing on things that are truly needed for the business, it makes it easier to stay clear of unnecessary expenses. Simply put, do not buy things because "monkey see, monkey do."

Don't stick to the sticker price. Ask for a discount! What's the worst that could happen? The seller says no, right? Always ask for a price lower than what is listed. If they counter offer, you still come out with a deal less than sticker price.

Keep office space to a bare minimum. Don't waste money on getting the suite in the downtown office building. If you truly need an office space, all major cities have shared working spaces for entrepreneurs that are often times free or at low cost. If you are a new entrepreneur, working in a shared workspace is great to foster community and collaboration.

Create systems.
Finding ways to automate items in your business will allow you to predict more of your costs.

Outsource. I am a firm believer in outsourcing things that cost you time. It's great to pursue DIY projects. However, spending days, weeks or months on non-revenue generating activities is definitely costing you money.

Separate your marketing dollars.
If you run a Facebook, Instagram and email campaign, send each audience to a different URL. This makes it easy to track which marketing method generates the most.

Bootstrapping Tips for Entrepreneurs:

Try swapping equity for expertise.

Test the market in small ways.

Looking to market something new but don't want to sink dollars into a big research project? Consider testing the minimum viable product, or micro testing. The idea is to develop something with the minimum number of features or information needed to gauge the marketability of a product online. That might mean mocking up a website with potential features and seeing how many visitors click on the item. It might also involve buying pay-per-click ads to see how easy it is to gain potential customers. It might mean selling a few products on a site like eBay to see how well they perform, before ordering in bulk from a wholesaler. What sets this approach apart from practices like using focus groups is that companies base product development decisions not just on what customers say they want, but on how they vote with their wallets.

Employ creative bartering.
Another $1,900 in barter dollars went to have the vehicle covered with his company's logo. Now the car functions

as a rolling billboard for People's Choice, and Sarantakis never misses a chance to drive it through town where curious crowds snap his photograph.

Encourage developers to jump in for free.
In March, Etsy, the online retail shop conglomerate that specializes in handmade and vintage goods, launched a set of programming tools that makes it easier for outside developers to build new applications using Etsy's code. By April, hundreds of programmers had registered to use it, and some 50 were working on new applications. By May, a developer, Daniel Dickison, had created an iPhone application called Etsy Addict. Customers downloaded Etsy Addict 1,600 times in its first month. The 99-cent fee is shared between Dickison and Apple. Etsy's then CEO, Maria Thomas, said the company had no problem with developers reaping the rewards of their work.

Manage your own public relations like a pro.
At start-ups, founders often wear many hats, including that of a PR manager. The good news is that reporters and bloggers are more likely to listen to a pitch from a company founder than a PR rep. "It means something when you tell somebody, 'I invented this product,'" says Leslie Haywood, founder of Charmed Life Products, a Charleston, South Carolina maker of grilling accessories. "They want to hear your story." J.J. McCorvey and April Joyner compiled an assortment of tips on how to reach out to the press, including starting small by contacting local media outlets or blogs, making a press list and knowing what the reporters you pitch write about.

Watch your competitors.
"Keeping track of who your competitors are, what people are saying about them, and what they are saying themselves can help you differentiate your business and stay

ahead of trends that could impact your business," says Michele Levy, an independent brand strategy consultant. You can do the research yourself by knowing the products or services your competitors sell, but there are also specialized tools you can tap into along the way.

Get Creative with new investment styles.

Keep your website simple and grow it organically.

Need IT? Get it virtually

Get free apps for that.
Some of the best Apple applications for business are free.
The $499 price tag on one model of the iPad might max out your credit card if you buy a couple, but it won't cause you to go running to investors. Check out web conferencing apps for iPad, which is a conference call tool that allows for brainstorming sessions and presentation sharing. It lets data

be shared in real-time and makes meetings portable. There's also Square, a free app that allows businesses to securely accept both cash and credit-card payments on the spot. The app will generate an email or text message to confirm the transaction.

Get your name out by getting outside.

When your hobby, be it block-printing stationery, crafting goat-milk soaps or designing upcycled lighting fixtures, shows enough promise to justify renting a stall, selling at a local flea market could be worth a shot. Most street fairs and markets have a very low barrier to entry: You'll need transit, a table, a tent (for outdoor markets), a cash box and the means to cover a small booth rental fee (usually $25 to $50 for small communities and $75-$125 for urban fairs). If your community doesn't have a flea market, look for seasonal markets or even neighborhood street fairs. Even if you're already successfully hawking your wares online, making periodic appearances at craft fairs, art shows, and flea markets can give your business new insight into the market, your regional competition, and local consumers' evolving desires.

Let your buyers and celebs create your buzz.
In the fall of 2000, Henri Bendel hosted a press breakfast to introduce 20 new suppliers. Maureen Kelly, who'd just started Tarte Cosmetics, found herself in a room buzzing with fashion magazine glitterati, many of whom subsequently wrote about Tarte. That exposure brought orders from national boutiques, including Bergdorf Goodman. After that, fashion magazines did Kelly's advertising for her. Her only promotional expense was using the website WhoRepresents.com to identify agents for celebrities and mail them samples. Oprah Winfrey was one target; in March 2001, Tarte turned up on the influential O List. For entrepreneurs

who may not be in Hollywood, utilizing social media "celebs" are a great way to get your brand out there.

Get creative with branding and marketing.

If you don't have the money to put major marketing dollars into your company, get creative. In launching Madsoul in 2000, an urban streetwear label, Marc D'Amelio raised guerrilla marketing to an art form. Take, for example, his sticker campaign. D'Amelio figured out that if he signed up for a United Parcel Service account, he was entitled to an unlimited supply of blank UPS labels. If he bought a Tektronix printer, he was entitled to free black ink. So, he signed on with both companies and began printing stickers by the thousands and distributing them at concerts and art festivals around New York City where Madsoul is based. "If you can't afford to do a $100,000 billboard, and you can't even afford to do a $20,000 print advertisement, you must figure out other ways," he said.

Chapter 9
DOOR NUMBER 3- CREATIVITY

Here are a few more creative ways to get your business going. This section will be geared more toward product-based businesses. The suggestions below are for people who are okay with starting small and growing to something larger.

1. Food Service

If you have desire to own a restaurant, you may not have the money (sometimes $1 million plus) to put into building, staff, equipment and food costs. A couple reasons food trucks are considered a low-cost business is that you don't need to sign a lease for a single restaurant location and can get by with few employees if you plan to manage the day-to-day operations yourself. These advantages are true, but that doesn't mean there won't be overhead.

Below are some great resources dedicated to the food truck biz:

Food Truck Empire Owner Brett Lindenberg has restaurant experience and has grown a community of food truck owners to be a resource for each other. :foodtruckempire.com

Food Truck Laws - No need in going to jail or getting fined. www.foodtrucklaws.com

Food Truck Row - Owners connecting with each other. www.foodtruckrow.com

One of the first steps that many food truck owners need to follow through with once they have started researching for their future rolling business is to find a commissary or commercial kitchen for their truck to call home.

Most municipalities throughout the country require that a mobile food unit be parked at and their food storage handled by a state licensed commercial kitchen. In addition to this, in the few cities where cooking is not allowed on the truck, the cooking and packaging of the food must also take place at the commissary.

Just as your vehicle is required to maintain local health standards, these commercial kitchens must also follow these rules. Please note that if a commercial kitchen loses its certification from the city or state, your truck will be grounded until the kitchen makes the needed corrections or you find a new home for your truck.

Shared kitchen spaces are another option because cooking is another field in which equipment can be very expensive. Sharing is a great idea for caterers and producers of artisan or other specialty foods. Perhaps you are a bread baker selling to local organic food stores and your best friend from cooking school makes cookies that she sells to individual consumers on her website. You could rent a commercial kitchen space together and, with the right type and size of oven for your needs, agree on a schedule and split the cost of rent and utilities.

You can also join a shared commercial kitchen. These are available in larger metropolitan areas. Many such kitchens are sponsored by "incubator" programs, which provide resources and work space to small start-up businesses. These kitchens have the advantage of being already licensed by the health department, so you don't need to worry about that regulatory hurdle. They provide all the necessary equipment and you schedule time as needed. Most allow you to do anything there: cook, teach a cooking class, or even film a cooking video.

For most caterers who are fresh in the game, a shared commercial kitchen is the most viable option. A shared-use kitchen is leased out to multiple caterers or chefs at once. Sharing the lease with other businesses means you'll save money, but scheduling can be an issue.

Finding a commercial kitchen that works for you is an integral part of bringing your gourmet mobile food to life. The location, type and size of your commercial kitchen will determine a lot of aspects of your business, including the type of dishes you can make, the capacity of events you can handle and where they can be located. When looking for a commissary or commercial kitchen, you can direct your search by the type of food you want to make and the scale of your operation.

The following are some commercial kitchen options:

Shared Commercial Kitchen - For most new food truck owners, a shared commercial kitchen is the most viable option. A shared-use kitchen is leased out to multiple caterers or chefs at once. It is a group kitchen for foodservice professionals. Because you share the lease with other businesses, you will save a lot of money like this, but if you and a co-renter want to schedule the space at the same time, you can have problems.

Private Commercial Kitchen - Leasing out your own private commercial kitchen space is the best option for a food truck business with large-scale aspirations. The benefits of having your own kitchen are endless. You do not have to worry about kitchen availability and you can purchase or lease your own equipment to ensure that you have everything you need to execute your menu on a large scale. If your space has a front of the house, you can also offer followers a tasting straight from your kitchen. Even better, if things go well, you can expand your carry-out and pick-up services, or start selling some of your signature items retail.

Restaurant Kitchen - Many food truck owners have found that renting out a restaurant kitchen during hours when the restaurant is closed is the most viable option for them. You will save money by leasing a space that would otherwise go unused during those hours. Furthermore, you will know exactly when you can use the kitchen and when you cannot, avoiding the scheduling issues that can occur with a shared-lease kitchen.

Some other options include schools, churches, and even the local VFW or Elk's Club. They may have inspected and certified commercial kitchens which can be rented, or even in some cases used as long as you sign an agreement to cater events for these organization as a means of payment or donation.

Once you know what kind of kitchen you want, you can start shopping around to find the best pricing and amenities for your commercial kitchen. One great tip to follow is to speak with other local food truck operators to find out which commissary or commercial kitchen they use. Some may or may not suggest using their current kitchen, but at least you can find out the current rates in your area. Your local health department can provide you with a list of the registered commercial kitchens in your area. Some municipalities have even started providing these lists on their websites.

Resources:
Culinary Incubator:
www.culinaryincubator.com/maps.php
Commercial Kitchen for Rent:
www.commercialkitchenforrent.com

Depending on your state, you may be able to legally operate your food business from home. Because these laws vary by state, you will have to check with your local city officials.

Private Label

Private label (also known as white label) works for just about every industry, including food (Bush's baked beans vs Walmart's Great Value baked beans). Private labels are a great way for independent retailers to compete against national chains and increase shopper loyalty. According to this special report published in December 2011 by Symphony IRI Group, prices for private labels can be up to 30% cheaper than national or global brands, which means a higher value for retailers and shoppers.

When it comes to beauty products, white label is the way to go. Quantity is the name of the game.

Other advantages of creating your own private label product include:

Attracting trendsetters and curious shoppers who want something different.

Having a product that reflects your overall brand identity.

Differentiating your business from the competition.

Although you can do a private label for just about any product, I choose to mention it under beauty products because that is the most popular in the market right now. However, anyone reading this looking to come out with their own line of black beans, the same rules apply.

Here is a great YouTube video of Mr. Miller, who owns a private label manufacturing company. It will give you a good idea of what private label is: http://bit.do/label

Featured in this Video- Steve Gabels

Gabel's Cosmetics 126 South Avenue 18 Los Angeles, CA 90031 (323)221-2430   Fax:(323)221-5911 steve@gabels.com

Cosmetic Index – Top 25 cosmetic private label manufacturer www.cosmeticindex.com

Food products private label – Private label food brands are a $90 billion business, accounting for 17.4 percent of retail food sales in the U.S. according to Nielsen Co. Over the past six years, while most food categories have been struggling, private labels have grown at a rate of 6 percent per year.

Private label manufacturers Association – www.plma.com/
Other types of private label products. Amazon has been doing private-label home gear for more than two years, under brands like Pinzon kitchen gadgets, Strathwood outdoor furniture, Pike Street bath and home products, and Denali tools.

You're a private label, health conscious, organic foods, fitness program. You can even sell event tickets under a private label!

Selling Your Products Wholesale
In addition to selling to customers, it may be wise to add a revenue stream

to your business. Wholesaling your product may be a way to make more money and eventually control your production expenses.

Don't be afraid to go after the big retailers early in the game. This is a particularly good strategy if they have a supplier diversity program that you qualify for. Although a lot of variables come into play when it comes to a buyer making a decision about including your product in their assortment, at the end of the day, it really boils down to whether they like your product or not. The buyer that happens to love your product could work for Walmart or a local mom and pop, so I recommend going after big and small retailers simultaneously. Usually it takes a bit longer to secure the buyer appointment with the larger retailers. So, while you are waiting for that appointment, you build your sales history with the individually owned and operated retailers where you can get your product in a lot faster.

The Key Is Quality
The most effective quality I have found to sell to retail stores is persistence. One must call on established and new accounts via direct mail, email and phone on a regular basis

Your wholesale business can experience the most growth by exhibiting at select trade shows that deliver high volume qualified traffic and then engaging prospective wholesale customers with passionate enthusiasm for your product. Our best tip to sell to retail stores if you don't have the funds to travel around to every trade show (which is normal), is to find the trade show that makes the most sense for your products and the types of buyers you are looking for. Attend so you can not only gain orders right away, but you will hopefully leave with several warm leads. You can also get a buyer attendee list that you can begin following up on as soon as you arrive back home. Trade shows are also a great way to network with other manufacturers and share resources. Aside from trade shows (because not all may be worth your time and money), we make spreadsheets with all of the retailers we would like to target. We then start going down the list and reach out. Don't get frustrated. This process can be deflating at times but persistence does pay off!

Develop a distribution network for your products. Depending on your product and its use, your distribution network may be retail establishments and or retail service providers that may use your product in their business. By establishing a distribution network, you will expand your footprint and develop a sales force for your products without having to directly pay for the sales. Offering a multi-tiered distribution program that rewards a distributor with lower wholesale prices based on the amount of product sold can help create incentives for the distributors to use products.

Chapter 10
LET'S WIN TOGETHER

When I look back at the times that I've failed, they don't bother me anymore, because I know that they were learning experiences. Everything that I've learned helped me to be able to do more. Instead of "What if?" constantly being on my mind, I now know how to take the lesson from each failure and move on to the next success. I ask myself now, "What if I had never tried it all? How much of a failure would that have been?"

I encourage you to know how personal finance works in your life and in your business. I want to teach you how to be mindful and, as you do that, you will be able to succeed. Whenever you fail, you will know how to be able to get up and move on to the next success in your business. Ignore that voice in your head that tells you it's easier to do something else. Ignore the thought that it is not a good idea and that you will not succeed. "Who's going to buy this? Who's actually going to care? Who's actually going to listen to me?" Well, I care! If I'm all you got, then so be it. We'll win together.

SMALL BUSINESS FINANCE GLOSSARY

Glossary Source: smallbusiness.house.gov/resources/glossary.htm

ACCOUNTS PAYABLE - Trade accounts of businesses representing obligations to pay for goods and services received.

ACCOUNTS RECEIVABLE - Trade accounts of businesses representing moneys due for goods sold or services rendered evidenced by notes, statements, invoices or other written evidence of a present obligation.

AFFILIATES - Business concerns, organizations, or individuals that control each other or that are controlled by a third party. Control may include shared management or ownership; common use of facilities, equipment, and employees; or family interest. The calculation of a firm's size includes the employees or receipts of all affiliates. Affiliation with another business concern is based on the power to control, whether exercised or not. Such factors as common ownership, common management and identity of interest (often found in members of the same family), among others, are indicators of affiliation. Power to control exists when a party or parties have 50 percent or more ownership. It may also exist with considerably less than 50 percent ownership by contractual arrangement or when one or more parties own a large share compared to other parties. The affiliated business concerns need not be in the same line of business.

AMORTIZATION - Gradual reduction of term debt by periodic payment sufficient to pay current interest and to eliminate the principal at maturity.

ANNUAL RECEIPTS - Receipts are averaged over a firm's latest 3 completed fiscal years to determine its average annual receipts. "Receipts" means the firm's gross or total income, plus cost of goods sold, as defined by or reported on the firm's Federal Income Tax return. The term does not include, however, net capital gains or losses, nor taxes collected for and remitted to a taxing authority if included in gross or total income. The firm may not deduct income taxes, property taxes, and cost of materials or funds paid to subcontractors. Travel, real estate and advertising agents, providers of conference management services, freight forwarders and customs brokers may deduct amounts they collect on behalf of another. If a firm has not been in business for 3 years, the average weekly receipts for the number of weeks the firm has been in business is multiplied by 52 to determine its average annual receipts.

ASSETS - The entire property of a person, association, corporation, or estate applicable or subject to the payment of debts.

BAD DEBTS - Funds owing to a business which are determined to be uncollectible.

BALANCE SHEET - Financial statement listing a company's assets, liabilities, and equity on a specific date.

BANKRUPTCY - A condition in which a business cannot meet its debt obligations and petitions a federal district court for either reorganization of its debts or liquidation of its assets. In the action the property of a debtor is taken over by a receiver or trustee in bankruptcy for the benefit of the creditors. This action is conducted as prescribed by the National Bankruptcy Act, and may be voluntary or involuntary.

BOOK VALUE - The value of an item or property at a specific time after deducting depreciation from original cost.

BREAK-EVEN POINT - The break-even point in any business is that point at which the volume of sales or revenues exactly equals total expenses -- the point at which there is neither a profit nor loss– under varying levels of activity. The break-even point tells the manager what level of output or activity is required before the firm can make a profit; reflects the relationship between costs, volume and profits.

BUSINESS BIRTH - Formation of a new establishment or enterprise.

BUSINESS CONCERN - A business concern eligible for assistance as a small business is a business entity organized for profit, with a place of business located in the United States, and which operates primarily within the United States or makes a significant contribution to the US economy through payment of taxes or use of American products, materials, or labor.

BUSINESS DEATH - Voluntary or involuntary closure of a firm or establishment.

BUSINESS DISSOLUTION - For enumeration purposes, the absence from any current record of a business that was present in a prior time period.

BUSINESS FAILURE - The closure of a business causing a loss to at least one creditor.

CAPACITY TO REPAY - The determination made by a lender on whether a borrower can repay a loan after examining financial statements, financial ratios and operating data.

CAPITAL - 1. Assets less liabilities, representing the ownership interest in a business; 2. A stock of accumulated goods, especially at a specified time and in contrast to income received during a specified time period; 3. Accumulated goods devoted to the production of goods; 4. accumulated possessions calculated to bring income.

CAPITAL EXPENDITURES - Business spending on additional plant equipment.

CAPITALIZATION - The basic resources of a company including the owner's equity, retained
earnings and fixed assets. One of the "Five C's" of Credit

CAP LINES LOAN PROGRAM - CAPLines is the umbrella program under which the SBA helps small businesses meet their short-term and cyclical working-capital needs.

CARRYING COSTS - Inventory costs associated with capital, storage, handling expenses, insurance, taxes and obsolescence.

CASH CONVERSION CYCLE - The length of time between the payment of payables and the collection of receivables.

CASH FLOW - The movement of money into and out of your business.

CASH FLOW STATEMENT - An accounting presentation showing how much of the cash generated by the business remains after both expenses (including interest) and principal repayment on financing are paid. A projected cash flow statement indicates whether the business will have cash to pay its expenses, loans, and make a profit. Cash flows can be calculated for any given period of time, normally done on a monthly basis. Also, one of the Five "Cs" evaluated in determining a loan applicant's credit-worthiness

CAWBO - Contract Assistance for Women Business Owners - The Office of Federal Contract

Assistance for Women Business Owners (CAWBO) was established October 1, 2000, in the Office of Government Contracting at the U.S. Small Business Administration. The purpose of the office is to increase federal contracting opportunities for women-owned small business (WOSB) and to increase the number of WOSB that successfully compete in the federal marketplace.

CDC - CERTIFIED DEVELOPMENT COMPANY - The 504 Certified Development Company (CDC) Program provides growing businesses with long-term, fixed-rate financing for major fixed assets, such as land and buildings. A Certified Development Company is a nonprofit corporation set up to contribute to the economic development of its community. CDCs work with the SBA and private - sector lenders to provide financing to small businesses. There are about 270 CDCs nationwide. Each CDC covers a specific geographic area.

CERTIFICATE OF COMPETENCY – COC -(SBA) - A certificate issued by the Small Business Administration (SBA) stating that the holder is "responsible" (in terms of capability, competency, capacity, credit, integrity, perseverance, and tenacity) for the purpose of receiving and performing a specific government contract.

CERTIFICATE OF DEPOSIT - Short-term instruments issued by commercial banks.

CERTIFICATION(s) or QUALIFICATION(s) REQUIREMENT(s) - "Certification" as a small business, as a socially and economically disadvantaged small business, as a woman-owned or veteran-owned business is required to be eligible for some SBA programs.

CERTIFIED 8(a) FIRM-(SBA) - A firm owned and operated by socially and economically disadvantaged individuals and eligible to receive federal contracts under the Small Business Administration's 8(a) Business Development Program.

CHARACTER - The degree to which a potential borrower feels a moral obligation to repay debts as evidenced by the borrower's credit and payment history. One of the "Five Cs" used in a lending officer's determination of a particular loan applicant's credit-worthiness.

CHARGED OFF LOAN - An uncollectible loan for which the principal and accrued interests were removed from the receivable accounts.

CHARGE-OFF - An accounting transaction removing an uncollectible balance from the active receivable accounts.

CLOSED LOAN - Any loan for which funds have been disbursed, and all required documentation has been executed, received and reviewed. For statistical purposes, first or total disbursement is counted as a closed loan.

CLOSING - Actions and procedures required to effect the documentation and disbursement of loan funds after the application has been approved, and the execution of all required documentation and its filing and recordation where required.

CLP - CERTIFIED LENDER PROGRAM – The most active and expert lenders qualify for the SBA's streamlined lending programs. Under these programs, lenders are delegated partial or full authority to approve loans, which results in faster service from SBA. Certified lenders are those who have been heavily involved in regular SBA loan-guaranty processing and have met certain other criteria. They receive a partial delegation of authority and are given a three-day turnaround by the SBA on their applications (they may also use regular SBA loan processing). Certified lenders account for nearly a third of all SBA business loan guaranties.

COC - Certificate of Competency- (SBA) - The Certificate of Competency (COC) program allows a small business to appeal a contracting officer's determination that it is unable to fulfill the requirements of a specific government contract on which it is the apparent low bidder. When the small business applies for a COC, SBA industrial and financial specialists conduct a detailed review of the firm's capabilities to perform on the contract. If the business demonstrates the ability to perform, the SBA issues a COC to the contracting officer requiring the award of that specific contract to the small business.

COLLATERAL - Something of value--securities, evidence of deposit or other property--pledged to support the repayment of an obligation. Also one of the Five "Cs" used in determining a loan
applicant's credit worthiness.

COLLECTION POLICY - Actions a business takes to collect slow-paying accounts.

COMMERCIAL PAPER - Unsecured promissory notes of large corporations.

COMMUNITY ADJUSTMENT AND INVESTMENT PROGRAM (CAIP) - (SBA) - The United States Community Adjustment and Investment Program was created to help communities that suffered job losses due to changing trade patterns with Mexico and Canada following the North American Free Trade Agreement (NAFTA). The CAIP promotes economic implementation of the adjustment by increasing the availability and flow of credit and encourages business development and expansion in impacted areas. Through the CAIP, credit is available to businesses in eligible communities to create new, sustainable jobs or to preserve existing jobs. The CAIP works with the

SBA in both their 7(a) Loan Guarantee Program and 504 Program to reduce borrower costs and increase the availability of these proven business assistance programs.

COMMUNITY EXPRESS-(SBA) - Community Express is a pilot SBA loan program that was developed in collaboration with the National Community Reinvestment Coalition (NCRC) and its member organizations. Under the pilot, which is available to selected lenders, a SBA Express like program will be offered to pre - designated geographic areas serving mostly New Markets small businesses. The program will also include technical and management assistance, which is designed to help increase the loan applicant's chances of success.

COMPROMISE - The settlement of a claim resulting from a defaulted loan for less than the full
amount due. Compromise settlement is a procedure available for use o only in instances where the government

cannot collect the full amount due within a reasonable time, by enforced collection proceedings or where the cost of such proceedings would not justify such effort.

CONDITIONS - External factors such as government regulation, competition, industry trends, and national economic trends can affect the success of a business. One of the "Five Cs" of credit.

CONSORTIUM - A coalition of organizations, such as banks and corporations, set up to fund ventures requiring large capital resources.

CONTINGENCY FUND - Cash held for emergencies or unexpected outflows of funds. Also known as "Precautionary Balances."

CONTRACT - A mutually binding legal relationship obligating the seller to furnish supplies or services (including construction) and the buyer to pay for them.

CONTRACTING - Purchasing, renting, leasing, or otherwise obtaining supplies or services from nonfederal sources. Contracting includes the description of supplies and services required, the selection and solicitation of sources, the preparation and award of contracts, and all phases of contract administration. It does not include grants or cooperative agreements.

COPYRIGHT - The legal right granted to authors, composers, artists and publishers to protect their thoughts and ideas for exclusive publication, reproduction, sale and distribution of their works. Some of the material on SBA's web site is copyrighted and it will be so stated in the document. If it is not Copyrighted we prefer that you link to our information rather than taking it and posting it on your site. Our information changes hourly and daily.

CORPORATION - A group of persons granted a state charter legally recognizing them as a separate entity having its own rights, privileges, and liabilities distinct from those of its members. The process of incorporating, should be completed with the state's secretary of state or state corporate counsel and usually requires the services of an attorney.

COSTS - Money obligated for goods and services received during a given period of time, regardless of when ordered or whether paid for.

CREDIT - Time allowed for the payment of goods or services sold on trust as well as confidence in the buyer's ability and intention to fulfill their financial obligations.

CREDIT PERIOD - Length of time allowed before the credit buyer must pay for credit purchases.

CREDIT POLICY - Actions taken by a business to grant, monitor and collect the cash for outstanding accounts receivable.

CREDIT RATING - A grade assigned to a business concern to denote the net worth and credit
standing to which the concern is entitled in the opinion of the rating agency as a result of its
investigation.

CURRENT ASSETS - Money, inventory and equipment that will be used up in the short term --
usually within one year.

DEBENTURE - Debt instrument evidencing the holder's right to receive interest and principal
installments from the named obligor. Applies to all forms of unsecured, long-term debt evidenced by a certificate of debt.

DEBT CAPITAL - Business financing that normally requires periodic interest payments and repayment of the principal within a specified time.

DEBT FINANCING - The provision of long term loans to small business concerns in exchange for debt securities or a note.

DEED OF TRUST - A document under seal which, when delivered, transfers a present interest in property. May be held as collateral.

DEFAULTS - The nonpayment of principal and/or interest on the due date as provided by the terms and conditions of the note.

DEFERRED LOAN - Loans whose principal and or interest installments are postponed for a specified period of time.

DEPRECIATION SCHEDULE - An accounting procedure for determining the amount of value left in a piece of equipment.

DISBURSEMENT - The actual payout to borrower of loan funds, in whole or part. It may be
concurrent with the closing, or follow it.

DISBURSING OFFICER - An employee authorized to pay out cash or issue checks in settlement of vouchers approved by a certifying officer.

DISCLAIMER - A statement regarding the responsibility and liability for website content and certain presenters, contractors, speakers, etc. Choosing "More..." at the end of this definition will lead you to SBA's Disclaimer Of Endorsement and Liability regarding the material in the upcoming viewing screens.

DISCOUNT INTEREST RATE - One in which the amount of interest is deducted from the face value of the loan with the borrower receiving the remainder.

DIVESTITURE - Change of ownership and/or control of a business from a majority (non-disadvantaged) to disadvantaged persons.

DUNS - Data Universal Numbering System - D&B's Data Universal Numbering System, the D&B DU-N-S Number, has become the standard for keeping track of the world's businesses. The D&B D-U-NS. Number is D&B's distinctive nine-digit identification sequence, which identifies information products and services originating exclusively through D&B. The D&B D-U-N-S Number is an internationally recognized common company identifier in EDI and global electronic commerce transactions. The world's most influential standards-setting organizations, more than 50 global, industry and trade associations, and the U.S. Federal Government recognize, recommend and/or require the D&B D-U-NS Number.

EARNING POWER - The demonstrated ability of a business to earn a profit, over time, while
following good accounting practices. When a business shows a reasonable profit on invested capital after fully maintaining the business property, appropriately compensating its owner and employees, servicing its obligations, and fully recognizing its costs, the business may be said to have demonstrated earning power. Demonstrated earning power is the foremost test of the business risk in pressing upon an application for a loan.

EMPLOYEES - The number of employees of a firm is its average number of persons employed for each pay period over the firm's latest 12 months. Any person on the payroll must be included as one employee regardless of hours worked or temporary status. The number of employees of a firm in business under 12 months is based on the average for each pay period it has been in business.

EQUITY - An accounting term used to describe the net investment of owners or stockholders in a business. Under the accounting equation, equity also represents the result of assets less liabilities.

EQUITY FINANCING - The provision of funds for capital or operating expenses in exchange for capital stock, stock purchase warrants and options in the business financed, without any guaranteed return, but with the opportunity to share in the company's profits. Equity financing includes long-term subordinated securities containing stock options and/or warrants. Utilized in SBIC financing activities.

EQUITY PARTNERSHIP - A limited partnership arrangement for providing start-up and seed capital to businesses.

ESCROW ACCOUNTS - Funds placed in trust with a third party, by a borrower for a specific purpose and to be delivered to the borrower only upon the fulfillment of certain conditions.

FAIR AND REASONABLE PRICE - A price that is fair to both parties, considering the agreed-upon conditions, promised quality, and timeliness of contract performance. "Fair and reasonable" price is subject to statutory and regulatory limitations.

FAIR MARKET VALUE - What a qualified buyer will pay for goods, services, or property.

FINANCIAL FORECAST - Projection of revenues and expenses for the next one to five years.

FINANCIAL RATIOS - Measures of capital, including debt to asset, current, and debt to worth. See individual definitions for "acid," "current," "quick" ratios.

FINANCIAL REPORTS - Reports commonly required from applicants request for financial assistance, e.g.: Balance Sheet -A report of the status of a firm's assets, liabilities and owner's equity at a given time.

FINANCING - New funds provided to a business, by either loans or purchase of debt securities or capital stock.

FIVE "Cs" OF CREDIT - A system used by lending officers to evaluate a loan application: Character, Cash Flow, Collateral, Capitalization and Conditions. See individual definitions.

FIXED ASSETS - Equipment, buildings, etc., which are purchased and used for long-term purposes.

FIXED COSTS - Costs of doing business such as rent, utilities, depreciation, taxes, etc., that remain generally, the same regardless of the amount of sales of goods or services.

FORECLOSURE - The act by the mortgagee or trustee upon default, in the payment of interest or principal of a mortgage of enforcing payment of the debt by selling the underlying security.

GOODWILL - An intangible asset of a business that relates to a favorable relationship with
customers, and excess earning power.

GRANT - Money given to a business that does not need to be repaid.

GUARANTEED LOAN-(SBA) - A loan made and serviced by a lending institution under agreement that a governmental agency will purchase the guaranteed portion if the borrower defaults.

GUARANTY - Promise by an individual or organization to repay a loan in the event of default.

GUIDE TO SBA's DEFINITIONS OF SMALL BUSINESS-(SBA) - The U. S. Small Business
Administration n (SBA) has prepared a guide to assist the general public in understanding SBA's
definitions of a small business. They are termed "size standards," and represent the largest a firm can be and still be considered a small business. This guide provides general information on size standard requirements and also addresses most of the typical concerns of the public regarding the use of size standards.

HAZARD INSURANCE - Insurance required showing lender as loss payee covering certain risks on real and personal property used for securing loans.

HUBZone - Historically Underutilized Business Zones - Through the HUB zone Empowerment
Contracting program federal contracting opportunities are provided for qualified small businesses located

in distressed areas. Fostering the growth of these federal contractors as viable businesses, for the long term, helps to empower communities, create jobs, and attract private investment.

INCOME STATEMENT - Financial statement showing a company's sales, expense and net income or loss for a specific period of time.

INDEPENDENT AND QUALIFIED PUBLIC ACCOUNTANTS - Public accountants are independent when neither they nor any of their family has a material, direct or indirect financial interest in the borrower other than as an accountant. They are qualified, unless there is contrary evidence, when they are either (1) certified, licensed, or otherwise registered if so required by the state in which they work, or (2) have worked as a public accountant for at least five years and are accepted by SBA.

INDUSTRY - Concerns primarily engaged in the same kind of economic activity are classified in the same industry regardless of their types of ownership (such as sole p proprietorship, partnership or corporation).

INSOLVENCY - The inability of a borrower to meet financial obligations as they mature, or having insufficient assets to pay legal debts.

INSTALLMENT LOAN - One in which the amount of interest is added to the principal and repaid by the borrower in equal periodic payments.

INTEREST - An amount paid a lender for the use of funds.

INVENTORY - Merchandise that is purchased and/or produced and stored for eventual sale.

INVENTORY TURNOVER - How often the inventory is sold and replenished over the course of a year.

INVESTMENT BANKING - Businesses specializing in the formation of capital. This is done by outright purchase and sale of securities offered by the issuer, standby underwriting or "best efforts selling."

IRS - Internal Revenue Service - with our link going to their publications and notices

JOB DESCRIPTION - A written statement listing the elements of a particular job or occupation, e.g., purpose, duties, equipment used, qualifications, training, physical and mental demands, working conditions, etc.

JOINT VENTURE - In a joint venture both firms share, in some proportion, the responsibility and the profits or loss on a contract. They are considered affiliated (see "Affiliates," above) for the purpose of that contract. Normally, the revenues or the employees of both firms are added together to determine the size of a joint venture.

JUDGMENT - Judicial determination of the existence of indebtedness, or other legal liability.

LEASE - A contract between the owner (lessor) and the tenant (lessee) stating the conditions under which the tenant may occupy or use real estate or equipment. Terms usually include a specific period of time and a predetermined rate.

LEASE RATE - The period rental payment to a lessor for the use of assets. It may also be considered as the implicit interest rate in minimum lease payments.

LENDING INSTITUTION - Any institution, including a commercial bank, savings and loan association, commercial finance company, or other lender qualified to participate with SBA in the making of loans.

LESSEE - The user of equipment or property being leased.

LESSOR - The party to a lease agreement who has legal or tax title to equipment or property, who grants the lessee the right to use the equipment or property for the lease term, and who is entitled to the rental fees.

LIABILITY - Debt owed by the company such as bank loans or accounts payable.

LICENSE - BUSINESS REGISTRATION - Businesses are licensed and registered at local and state levels of government. Each state has their own mechanism or criteria for obtaining licenses.

LIEN - A charge upon or security interest in real or personal property maintained to ensure the
satisfaction of a debt or duty ordinarily arising by operation of law.

LINE OF CREDIT - A short-term loan, usually less than one year.

LIQUIDATION - The disposal, at maximum prices, of the collateral securing a loan, and the voluntary and enforced collection of the remaining loan balance from the obligators and/or guarantors.

LIQUIDATION VALUE - The net value realizable in the sale (ordinarily a forced sale) of a business or a particular asset.

LIQUID ASSETS - Cash, checks and easily-convertible securities available to meet immediate and emergency needs.

LITIGATION - Refers to a loan in "liquidation status" which has been referred attorneys for legal action. Also: The practice of taking legal action through the judicial process.

LOAN AGREEMENT - Agreement to be executed by borrower, containing pertinent terms, conditions, covenants and restrictions.

LOAN PAYOFF AMOUNT - The total amount of money needed to meet a borrower's obligation on a loan. It is arrived at by accruing gross interest for one day and multiplying this figure by the number of days that exist between the d ate of the last repayment and the date on which the loan is to be completely paid off. This amount, known as accrued interest, is combined with the latest principal and escrow balances that are applicable to what is now referred to as the loan payoff amount. In the case where prepaid interest exceeds the accrued interest the latter is subtracted from the former and the difference is used to reduce the total amount owed.

LONG TERM - Period usually greater than one year.

LOSS RATE - A rate developed by comparing the ratio of total loans charged off to the total loans disbursed from inception of the program to the present date.

MARKET - The existing or potential buyers for specific goods or services.

MARKET VALUE - What a willing buyer will pay for goods, services, a property or a business.

MARKETING - The total of activities involved in the transfer of goods and services from the producer or seller to the consumer or buyer. Marketing activities may include buying, storing selling, advertising, pricing and promoting products.

MATURITY - The date on which a loan becomes due.

MATURITY EXTENSIONS - Extensions of payment beyond the original period established for repayment of a loan.

MICRO LOAN PROGRAM - The Micro loan Program provides very small loans to start-up, newly established, or growing small business concerns. Under this program, SBA makes funds available to nonprofit community based lenders (intermediaries) which, in turn, make loans to eligible borrowers in amounts up to a maximum of $35,000. The average loan size is about $10,500. Applications are submitted to the local intermediary and all credit decisions are made on the NEGOTIATED GRIEVANCE PROCEDURE The sole and exclusive procedure available to all employees in a bargaining unit and the employer for processing grievances and disputes.

MORTGAGE - An instrument giving legal title to secure the repayment of a loan made by the
mortgagee (lender). In legal contemplation there are two types: (1) title theory -operates as a

transfer of the legal title of the property to the mortgagee, and (2) lien theory -creates a lien upon the property in favor of the mortgagee.

NEGATIVE NET WORTH - A business condition when total liabilities exceed total assets.

NET WORTH - Property owned (assets), minus debts and obligations owed (liabilities), is the owner's equity (net worth).

NEW MARKETS VENTURE CAPITAL - NMVC-(SBA) - The New Markets Venture Capital (NMVC) program is modeled after the Small Business Administration's extremely successful Small Business Investment Company (SBIC) program but has a specific mission of economic development in low- income (LI) areas. Through a combination of equity-type financing and intensive operational assistance to smaller businesses located in LI areas, the program seeks to assist local entrepreneurs, create quality employment opportunities for residents and build wealth within these communities. SBA intends to achieve these public policy objectives through financial assistance to newly formed NMVC companies and to existing Specialized Small Business Investment Companies (SSBICs).

NON-MANUFACTURER - For purposes of Federal government contracts, a firm that supplies a product it did not manufacture is termed a non-manufacturer. To qualify for Federal government contracting, a non-manufacturer must have 500 or fewer employees, be primarily in the wholesale or retail trade, and supply the product of a US small manufacturer. This requirement is called the "non-manufacturer rule." This rule does not apply to supply contracts of $25,000 or less that are processed under Simplified Acquisition Procedures. The requirement may also be waived through formal procedure by the Associate Administrator for Government Contracting if there is no small manufacturer in the Federal market for a class of products.

NORTH AMERICAN INDUSTRY CLASSIFICATION SYSTEM (NAICS) - The North American Industry Classification System (NAICS) is replacing the U.S. Standard Industrial Classification (SIC) system. NAICS will reshape the way we view our changing economy. NAICS was developed jointly by the U.S., Canada, and Mexico to provide new comparability in statistics about business activity across North America.

NOTES AND ACCOUNTS RECEIVABLE - A secured or unsecured receivable evidenced by a note or open account arising from activities involving liquidation and disposal of loan collateral.

OBLIGATIONS - Technically defined as "amount of orders placed, contracts awarded, services
received, and similar transactions during a given period which will

require payments during the same or a future period." Also, another term for debt: money, merchandise or service owed to someone.

OFFICE OF SMALL & DISADVANTAGED BUSINESS UTILIZATION (OSDBU) - (SBA) – Federal Offices of Small and Disadvantaged Business Utilization (OSDBUs) offer small business information on procurement opportunities, guidance on procurement procedures, and identification of both prime and subcontracting opportunities.

OHA - Office of Hearings and Appeals - The Office of Hearings and Appeals, an independent office of the Small Business Administration (SBA or Agency). It is composed of two offices, the Office of Hearings and Appeals (OHA), and the Freedom of Information/Privacy Acts (FOI/PA) Office. The Small Business Administration established the Office of Hearings and Appeals (OHA) in 1983 to provide an independent, quasi-judicial appeal of certain SBA program decisions. OHA succeeded the SBA Size Appeals Board. Over the years, the SBA has expanded OHA's mission.

ORDERING COSTS - Administrative costs of placing, tracking, shipping, receiving and paying for an order.

OSHA (OCCUPATIONAL SAFETY & HEALTH ACT) - To assure safe and healthful working conditions for working men and women; by authorizing enforcement of the standards developed under the Act; by assisting and encouraging the States in their efforts to assure safe and healthful working conditions; by providing for research, information, education, and training in the field of occupational safety and health; and for other purposes.

OUTLAYS - Net disbursements (cash payments in excess of cash receipts) for administrative

expenses and for loans and related costs and expenses (e.g., gross disbursements for loans and
expenses minus loan repayments, interest and fee income collected, and reimbursements received for services performed for other agencies).

PARTNERING - A mutually beneficial business-to-business relationship based on trust and
commitment and that enhances the capabilities of both parties.

PARTNERSHIP - A legal relationship existing between two or more persons contractually associated as joint principals in a business.

PATENT - A patent secures to an inventor the exclusive right to make, use and sell an invention for 17 years. Inventors should contact the U.S. Department of Commerce Patent Office.

PETTY CASH - A small fund maintained for incidental expenses.

PRECAUTIONARY BALANCES - Cash held for emergencies or unexpected outflows of funds. Also known as "contingency fund."

PREFERRED LENDER PROGRAM (PLP) - (SBA) - The most active and expert lenders qualify for the SBA's streamlined lending programs. Under these programs, lenders are delegated partial or full authority to approve loans, which results in faster service from SBA. Preferred lenders are chosen from among the SBA's best lenders and enjoy full delegation of lending authority in exchange for a lower rate of guaranty. This lending authority must be renewed at least every two years, and the lender's portfolio is examined by the SBA periodically. Preferred loans account for more than 10 percent of SBA loans.

PRIME - Program for Investment in Micro-entrepreneurs Act: The U.S. Small Business Administration plans to issue Federal grants awards to qualified organizations under PRIME to provide training and technical assistance to disadvantaged micro-entrepreneurs. These organizations include: non-profit micro-enterprise development organizations or programs; intermediaries; other micro-enterprise development organizations or programs that are accountable to a local community, working in conjunction with a State or local government or Indian tribe; or Indian tribes acting on their own, with proper certification that no other qualified organization exists within their jurisdiction.

PRIME CONTRACT - A contract awarded directly by the Federal government.

PRIME RATE - Interest rate which is charged business borrowers having the highest credit ratings, for short term borrowing. As published daily in the Wall Street Journal, it is the basis for rates to other lenders.

PROFESSIONAL AND TRADE ASSOCIATIONS - Non-profit, cooperative and voluntary organizations that are designed to help their members in dealing with problems of mutual interest. In many instances professional and trade associations enter into an agreement with SBA to provide volunteer counseling to the small business community.

PROPRIETORSHIP - The most common legal form of business ownership; about 85 percent of all small businesses are proprietorships. The liability of the owner is unlimited in this form of ownership.

QUICK RATIO - Current assets less inventories divided by current liabilities. Also called "acid ratio."

RATIO - The ratio of current assets to liabilities. Also called "quick ratio."

RETURN ON INVESTMENT - The amount of profit (return) based on the amount of resources (funds) used to produce it. Also, the ability of a given investment to earn a return for its use.

REVOLVING CREDIT ACCOUNT - A formal line of credit offered to larger businesses in exchange for up-front fees and standard interest payments.

SBA - Small Business Administration- (SBA) - An independent agency of the federal government and not to be confused with Small Business Association or variations thereof. The U.S. Small Business Administration (SBA) was created by Congress in 1953 to help America's entrepreneurs form successful small enterprises. Today, SBA's program offices in every state offer financing, training and advocacy for small firms. These programs are delivered by SBA offices in every state, the District of Columbia, the Virgin Islands and Puerto Rico. In addition, the SBA works with thousands of lending, educational and training institutions nationwide.

SBA EXPORT EXPRESS-(SBA) - SBA Export Express combines the SBA's small business lending assistance with its technical assistance programs to help small businesses that have traditionally had difficulty in obtaining adequate export financing. The pilot program is available throughout the country and is expected to run through September 30, 2005

SBA Express - The SBA Express - Makes it easier and faster for lenders to provide small business loans of $150,000 or less; allows lenders to use their own forms and processes to approve loans guaranteed by the U.S. Small Business Administration; provides a rapid response from the SBA - within 36 hours of receiving your complete application; lets lenders take advantage of electronic loan processing; and helps lenders provide smaller revolving loans.

SBA LOAN - The SBA enables its lending partners to provide financing to small businesses when funding is otherwise unavailable on reasonable terms by guaranteeing major portions of loans made to small businesses.

SBA LOWDOC - SBA Low-Doc - streamlines the making of small business loans. The maximum loan- $150,000. Calls for a response from the SBA within 36 hours of receiving a complete application. Guaranty percent follows 7(a) policy.

SBIC - Small Business Investment Company - Licensed by the Small Business Administration,
SBICs are privately owned and managed investment firms. They are participants in a vital partnership between government and the private sector economy. With their own capital and with funds borrowed at favorable rates through the Federal Government, SBICs provide venture capital to small independent businesses, both new and already

established. Selecting More... will take you to the SBIC (Office of Investment) home page.

SBIR CONTRACT - Small Business Innovative Research Contract - A type of contract designed
to foster technological innovation by small businesses with 500 or fewer employees. The SBIR contract program provides for a three-phased approach to research and development projects: technological feasibility and concept development; the primary research effort; and the conversion of the technology to a commercial application.

SCORE-(SBA) - SCORE is a 10,500-member volunteer association sponsored by the SBA.
SCORE matches volunteer business-management counselors with present prospective small-business owners in need of expert advice. The SCORE home page is located at www.score.org.

SECONDARY MARKET - Entities who purchase an interest in a loan from an original lender, such as banks, institutional investors, insurance companies, credit unions and pension funds. There is an active secondary market in the loans guaranteed by the Small Business Administration. This market was created to increase the attractiveness of small business lending to the lending community. Through the market, lenders are able to sell the guaranteed portion n of SBA guaranteed loans to investors and thereby improve their liquidity and increase their yield on the unguaranteed portion of SBA loans. In addition, the secondary market provides a hedge against future liquidity problems because the guaranteed portion n of an SBA guaranteed portfolio may be readily sold by the lender. The market also allows a lender to meet the credit needs of a local small business community by importing capital from other parts of the country.

SELLING A BUSINESS - Selling a business is different than selling any other asset because a business is more than an income-earning asset -- it is a life-style as well. Therefore, the decision to sell can be emotional. Personal ambitions should be weighed against economic consequences in reaching a decision.

SHORT TERM - Period usually one year or less.

SIMPLE INTEREST RATE LOAN - One which provides the borrower the face value of the loan; the borrower repays the principal plus interest at maturity.

SIZE STANDARDS - The term "size standard" describes the numerical definition of a small business. In other words, a business is considered "small" if it meets or is below an established "size standard." SMALL BUSINESS - A business smaller than a given size as measured by its employment, business receipts, or business assets.

SMALL BUSINESS ACT - See www.sba.gov/content/small-business-act

SMALL BUSINESS DEVELOPMENT CENTER (SBDC) - (SBA) - The SBDC is a center for the delivery of joint government, academic and private sector services for the benefit of small business and the national welfare. It is committed to the development and productivity of business and the economy in specific geographical regions. (See locations at www.sba.gov/gopher/LocalInformation/Small-Business-Development-Centers).

SMALL BUSINESS INVESTMENT ACT - It is declared to be the policy of the Congress and the purpose of this Act to improve and stimulate the national economy in general and the small-business segment thereof in particular by establishing a program to stimulate and supplement the flow of private equity capital and long-term loan funds which small-business concerns need for the sound financing of their business operations and for their growth, expansion, and modernization, and which are not available in adequate supply: Provided, however, That this policy shall be carried out in such manner as to insure the maximum participation of private financing sources.

SMALL BUSINESS INVESTMENT COMPANY (SBIC) - (SBA) - SBICs, licensed by the Small Business Administration, are privately owned and managed investment firms. They are participants in a vital partnership between government and the private sector economy. With their own capital and with funds borrowed at favorable rates through the Federal Government, SBICs provide venture capital to small independent businesses, both new and already established.

SMALL DISADVANTAGED BUSINESS (SDB) - SBA certifies SDBs to make them eligible for special bidding benefits. SDBs are at least 51 percent owned by one or more individuals who are both socially and economically disadvantaged. This can include a publicly owned business that has at least 51 percent of its stock unconditionally owned by one or more socially and economically disadvantaged individuals and whose management and daily business is controlled by one or more such individuals.

SMALL DISADVANTAGED BUSINESS CONCERN - A small business concern that is at least 51 percent owned by one or more individuals who are both socially and economically disadvantaged. This can include a publicly owned business that has at least 51 percent of its stock unconditionally owned by one or more socially and economically disadvantaged individuals and whose management and daily business is controlled by one or more such individuals.

SOLVENCY - The financial ability to continue business.

SOPs-(SBA) - SBA Standard Operating Procedures.

STANDARD INDUSTRIAL CLASSIFICATION (SIC) CODE - A code representing a category within the Standard Industrial Classification System administered by the Statistical Policy Division of the U.S. Office of Management and Budget. The system was established to classify all industries in the US economy. A two-digit code designates each major industry group, which is coupled with a second two-digit code representing subcategories.

STARTUP, or START UP or STARTUP KIT - SBA maintains a generic startup kit and in many cases, startup kits for beginning a business in given states.

SUBCONTRACT - A contract between a prime contractor and a subcontractor to furnish supplies or services for the performance of a prime contract or subcontract.

SURETY BOND - A three-way agreement between a surety company, a contractor and the project owner. If the contractor fails to comply with the contract, the surety assumes responsibility and ensures that the project is completed. By law, prime contractors to the federal government must post surety bonds on federal construction projects valued at $25,000 or more. Many state, county, city and private -sector projects require bonding as well. The SBA can guarantee bid, performance and payment bonds for contracts up to $1.25 million for small businesses that cannot obtain bonds through regular commercial channels. Bonds may be obtained in two ways: prior approval-- contractors apply through a surety bonding agent. The guaranty goes to the surety; and preferred Sureties-- preferred sureties are authorized by the SBA to issue, monitor and service bonds without prior SBA approval.

TAX or TAXES - The contribution required of persons, groups, or businesses within a governmental jurisdiction for the support of governmental programs. Springtime brings a flood of questions about State taxes. We have compiled a list of State sites and their specific tax rules and guidelines.

TRADE NAME - The term used to identify a company. Any type of business may call itself a company.

TRADEMARK - Words, names, symbols or devises, or any combination of these, used to identify the goods of a business and to distinguish these goods from the goods of others.

TREASURY BILLS - T-Bills - Short term obligations of the U.S. government.
TURNOVER - Turnover is the number of times that an average inventory of goods is sold during a fiscal year or

some designated period. Care must be taken to ensure that the average inventory and net sales are both reduced to the same denominator; that is, divide inventory at cost into sales at cost into sales at cost or divide inventory at selling price into sales at selling price. The turnover when accurately computed, is one measure of the efficiency of a business.

UNFAIR LABOR PRACTICE - Action by either the employer or the union which violates the
provisions of Executive Order 11491 as amended.

UNIFORM COMMERCIAL CODE - Codification of uniform laws concerning commercial transactions. In SBA parlance generally refers to a uniform method of recording and enforcing a security interest or charge upon existing or to be acquired personal property.

VARIABLE COSTS - Those costs of doing business such as cost of goods, shipping, handling and storage, sales commissions, etc., which are directly related to the sales of goods or services.

VENTURE CAPITAL - Money used to support new or unusual commercial undertakings; equity, risk or speculative capital. This funding is provided to new or existing firms that exhibit above -average growth rates, a significant potential for market expansion and the need for additional financing for business maintenance or expansion.

WBC - Women's Business Centers or Women's Business Center - Each women's business center
provides assistance and/or training in finance, management, marketing, procurement and the
Internet, as well addressing specialized topics such as home - based businesses, corporate executive downsizing and welfare -to-work. All

provide individual business counseling and access to the SBA's programs and services; a number are also intermediaries for the SBA's Microloan and Loan Pre-qualification programs. Each WBC tailors its programs to the needs of its constituency; many offer programs and counseling in two or more languages. The following is contact information and a brief description of each WBC. Choosing More... will take you to a complete listing.

WBOR - Women's Business Ownership Representatives - Representatives in SBA offices to
assist women business owners.

WORKING CAPITAL - Cash and short-term assets that can be used for current needs -- bills, etc.

www.ingramcontent.com/pod-product-compliance
Lightning Source LLC
Chambersburg PA
CBHW071422180526
45170CB00001B/182